———

This book attempts to explain how the great eighteenth-century architect Robert Adam went about the business of design. It therefore deals with Adam's drawings rather than the buildings themselves, and tries to show that these pen, wash and watercolour 'inventions', of which he was an acknowledged master, were the ideal vehicle for his architectural ideas first and last.

It was to this end that Robert and his brother James studied drawing and composition in the most advanced drawing schools of Rome. The Adam publication *The Works of Architecture* (1773) attempted an equation between drawing style, Robert Adam 'inventions' and the picturesque, which dominated the last twenty years of the Adam practice. *The Works* itself is seen as a seminal book which obliquely supplied the theory for the Adam interpretation of the picturesque in its various prefaces and the plates themselves. In all of this Adam was served by a carefully organised office, itself virtually a drawing academy.

———

CAMBRIDGE STUDIES IN THE HISTORY OF ARCHITECTURE

Robert Adam: drawings and imagination

CAMBRIDGE STUDIES IN THE HISTORY OF ARCHITECTURE

Edited by

ROBIN MIDDLETON
Professor of Art History, Columbia University

JOSEPH RYKWERT
Paul Philippe Cret Professor of Architecture, University of Philadelphia

and DAVID WATKIN
Reader in the History of Western Architecture, University of Cambridge, and Fellow of Peterhouse

THIS IS A NEW series of historical studies intended to embrace a wide chronological range, from antiquity to the twentieth century, and to become a natural counterpart to Cambridge Studies in the History of Art. Volumes in the series are meant primarily for professional historians of architecture and their students, but it is also hoped to include a number of volumes for course work or of interest to the general reader.

Titles in the series

French architects and engineers in the Age of the Enlightenment
ANTOINE PICON
Translated by MARTIN THOM

Sir James Pennethorne and the making of Victorian London
GEOFFREY TYACK

Robert Adam: drawings and imagination
A. A. TAIT

The Antique Architect, 1773

Robert Adam
drawings and
imagination

A. A. TAIT

Richmond Professor in the History of Art,
University of Glasgow

Published by the Press Syndicate of the University of Cambridge

The Pitt Building, Trumpington Street, Cambridge CB2 1RP

40 West 20th Street, New York, NY 10011–4211, USA

10 Stamford Road, Oakleigh, Melbourne 3166, Australia

First published 1993

Printed in Great Britain at the University Press, Cambridge

A catalogue record for this book is available from the British Library

Library of Congress cataloguing in publication data

Tait, A. A. (Alan Andrew), 1938–
Robert Adam: drawings and imagination / A. A. Tait.
p.   cm. – (Cambridge studies in the history of architecture)
Includes index.
ISBN 0 521 43315 0
1. Adam, Robert, 1728–1792 – Criticism and interpretation.
2. Architectural drawing – 18th century – England. 3. Picturesque,
The, in architecture. I. Adam, Robert, 1728–1792. II. Title.
III. Series.
NA2707.A3T35 1993
720'.22'22–dc20 92–47466 CIP

ISBN 0 521 43315 0 hardback

Contents

Colour illustrations

Illustrations

Preface

THERE ARE THREE holdings of Robert Adam's drawings, one larger than the other two. The first is the eight thousand or so drawings of all sizes and types, in the Sir John Soane's Museum, London, where they arrived in 1833. The other two were part of the Soane Collection, in the sense that they were originally intended for it and by accident remained in family hands, one in the Clerk of Penicuik Collection, at Penicuik House, and the other at Blair Adam, the familial repository. There are, of course, other drawings in various collections, and most public holdings have some Adam drawings of one kind or another. The Print Room of the Royal Museum of Fine Art, Copenhagen, has a virtually unique set of Adam classical *capricci*, the Pierpont Morgan Library, New York has an unfinished landscape Album by both Adam and his master Lallemand, and the Prints and Drawings Department of the National Gallery of Scotland has a remarkable holding of Robert Adam's picturesque inventions.

In looking at all these drawings and in writing this book, I have accumulated an enormous debt to their keepers. To the present and past Curators of the Sir John Soane's Museum, its Inspectresses and to Miss Christine Scull of the Students Room, I owe a great deal. They have been patient, unfailingly helpful and hospitable over more years than I care to remember. The same has been true of Sir John Clerk at Penicuik and Keith Adam at Blair Adam. In the Print Rooms of Edinburgh and Copenhagen both the Keepers have now departed, Keith Andrews from the former and Erik Fischer from the latter, as has Agnes Mongan from the Morgan Library.

My work has been most generously supported by the British Academy and the Leverhulme Trust, and the book itself by the Carnegie Trust for the Universities of Scotland. Like any historian, I am living on the works of others and such indebtedness was always a sensitive point with the brothers Adam. So it seems appropriate to dedicate this book to their memory – that is to the adelphi – τοῖς ἀδελφοῖς.

Photographic acknowledgements and abbreviations

Blair Adam Collection: 1, 2, 5, 12–14, 26, 28, 74, 76, 106–7, 113, 116, 132–3; Clerk of Penicuik Collection: 31; A. F. Kersting: 21; Private Collections: 3, 18, 41, 100, 114, 117; Earl of Rosebery: 38, 128; British Museum; 123, 136; National Galleries of Scotland: 8, 115, 124, 126, 135; National Library of Wales: 125; National Trust, Photographic Library: 77, 108, 111; Royal Commission on the Historical Monuments of England: 20; Sir John Soane's Museum, London: 4, 9, 11, 15–17, 24, 30, 34–5, 39, 40, 42–4, 46–8, 51–4, 56–8, 60–1, 63–70, 72–3, 75, 78–81, 87, 102–4, 109–110, 112, 118, 120, 127, 131, 138–143; University of Glasgow, Hunterian Art Gallery: 6, 10, 134; Library: 25, 27, 50, 55; Victoria and Albert Museum, Picture Library: 29, 33; Accademia Nazionale di San Luca, Rome: 32, 37; Archives Générales du Royaume de Belgique, Brussels: 22; Cooper-Hewitt Museum, New York: 49; Huntington Library, Art Collections, San Marino: 121–2; Musées de Marseille, Musée Grobet Labadie: 59; Pierpont Morgan Library, New York: 19; Statens Museum for Kunst, Copenhagen: 119; Yale Center for British Art: 129, 130.

Blair Adam Collection	This refers to a handlist of the drawings made in 1976 by the National Register of Archives (Scotland)
Soane Museum AV	Sir John Soane's Museum, London, Adam Volumes
SRO	Scottish Record Office, Edinburgh
The Ruins	Robert and James Adam, *The Ruins of the Palace of the Emperor Diocletian at Spalatro* (London, 1766)
The Works	Robert and James Adam, *The Works in Architecture of Robert and James Adam* 2 vols., (London, 1773–1779)

Introduction

IT MAY SEEM odd that a book about one of the greatest British architects should spend so little time dealing with his buildings. The whole thrust of what is termed architectural history has concerned itself largely with monuments and their relationship with one another. Architectural reputations have nonetheless been marked up or down according to such an architectural reading. However, for the brothers Adam, a different case can be made – different, largely because of the volume of visual material which has survived, unequalled in quality and quantity by any other eighteenth-century architect and offering a unique insight into the brothers' and their offices' methods of work. To concentrate on such sources, especially the drawings, and construct some sort of pattern from their architectural ideas and schemes seems to me as valid as looking at their buildings and divining a meaning from them.

To do this, I have dealt largely with the drawings themselves. Because of the importance I have assigned to them, I have tried to show something of the mechanics of drawing and those involved in making such a delicate and sensitive piece of machinery work. Though I have not ignored what might be termed the orthodox Adam drawing – usually a handsome, coloured elevation of an interior – I have concentrated on the freer, more casual seeming sketches, and particularly those called the picturesque inventions, of which, over a thousand have survived. It can be argued that these revealed, with unrivalled insight and intimacy, Robert Adam's conception of an architecture and landscape inseparably bonded together. It will be apparent too, that I have dealt, in this book, with the two brothers, that is to say Robert and his younger brother James, whom I have always referred to as James Adam for clarity's sake. This has been done because, until around 1773, the brothers worked very much as a team, though not of equals. *The Works in Architecture*, published by them in 1773, obviously marked such a collaboration where James Adam largely wrote and Robert Adam edited the text. After this, James Adam more or less retired from the architectural scene to the life of an agricultural economist on the Essex–

Hertfordshire borders. His *Practical Essays on Agriculture*, which appeared as two volumes in 1789, was probably intended to set a belated seal on such a career. In the post 1773 years – those of the picturesque – Robert Adam was alone in the direction of the Adam Office. The far-reaching stylistic changes made, in its architecture, during this period, must be laid unequivocably, at his door.

The chapters that follow are largely in chronological order. The first three deal almost exclusively with the years until 1773, when the first part of the brothers' *Works in Architecture* appeared in London. In them, I have concentrated on the brothers' visual and intellectual re-education in Italy on either side of 1760, and what they gained from such an experience in the broadest sense. Chapter 1 is particularly concerned with Robert Adam's time in Rome and the conflicting roles he assumed there, of the connoisseur and professional, and how such a self-imposed discipline of learning by stealth isolated him from his natural companions, and made both him and his brother unusually dependent and demanding of instructors, like Dewez, Lallemand and Clérisseau. Both brothers were acutely aware of their ambiguous roles and Robert ironically made clear that his industry had left James Adam with Rome 'to do as a gentleman would do for his pleasure'. Such attitudes go some way to explaining why both brothers stood aside from competing in the public, architectural prizes of the Roman *concorsi*. Instead, their mentors encouraged similar exercises with grandiose schemes for palaces and parliament houses, and even the rebuilding of Lisbon, as a sort of private substitute. The anti-establishment if not anti-academic feeling of the brothers' teachers, especially Clérisseau and Piranesi, may well have fanned their detachment and certainly rubbed off on the brothers. For later on in 1772, their assistant Antonio Zucchi was reported to have told Adam 'that the greatest men of Italy were not bred by the Academy' and this was intended to be music to the Adams' ears. All this is discussed in chapter 2. The reverse of the Adam disguise – the voracious collector and opinionated virtuoso – are closely looked at in the following chapter, where the cultural baggage of the Italian tours – paintings, drawings, antiquities and even in physical form draughtsmen like Dewez, Brunias and Sacco – were all established in Lower Grosvenor Street, each having, in turn, a part to play in the formation of the Adam style.

The Grosvenor Street house, possibly with its renaissance style octagon, was a vehicle for the display of the brothers' talents as well as their Old Masters and antiquities. The last two were their passport to cultural gentility and ever elusive financial gain while the first demonstrated a professional establishment of vigour and invention. Such an office, both here and, after 1771, at The Adelphi, was the heart of the Adam engine in which the Italian and Italian-inspired draughtsmen were the pistons. Chapter 3 looks at them and how they were organised within the office and the degree of independence they were permitted. In the cases of the principal draughtsmen like Richardson, Bonomi and the Robertsons this was considerable. Yet they were always and unmistakably directed and perhaps only the imported and colourful Manocchi powerfully influenced the development of the Adam style. Policy and its direction were always in the brothers' hands and after about 1775 in Robert's hands alone. All office drawings from sketch to finished sheet were inevitably theirs; as they put it in 1789, drawings were 'their stock in trade'. Such an acute sense of possession was understandable when it is recalled that drawing was Adam's first love and always remained so. His family had reported with slight exaggeration that 'hardly could this infant hold a pencil when he discovered through his childish production that in a riper season he would charm the world with those that should flow from it'.

The arrangement and character of the two following chapters, 4 and 5, perhaps need a little explanation. That which deals with the *Works in Architecture* – 4 – is of critical importance for it marks a turning point in the whole Adam style. The years following 1773 showed a waning of the cosmopolitan international manner so assiduously cultivated by the brothers in Rome and so successfully practised in the early years. In its stead, Adam developed an idiosyncratic variation on the fashionable style of the picturesque where building was regarded as part of scenery. As the several prefaces to *The Works* and the plates themselves make clear, the Adam interpretation of the picturesque had more to do with variety, colour and movement, all painterly qualities, than the conventional tools and techniques of architecture. Such a broad view had allowed Adam to judge his rival Sir William Chambers' architecture as 'more architectonic than picturesque' and this was not approbation. His interest had been aroused early, and even before his arrival in Italy, he showed a Rousseau-like enthusiasm for wild scenery and nature. How Adam turned so literary and pictorial a movement as the picturesque into architecture is the theme of chapter 5 whose documents are the endless essays in wash, tinting and watercolour relentlessly explored over the decade of the 1780s until the end in 1792.

There is little biographical material in these chapters and not much attempt has been made to fathom the brothers' natures, apart from where they themselves suggested a particular interpretation. In this fashion, the brothers and especially Robert Adam's architectural evolution has been seen through drawings rather than by quoting from letters or illustrating buildings. This has not been to deny in any way the extreme importance of such material, it is, as has been said, because my purpose is different. Much about their lives and letters can be easily found in John Fleming's *Robert Adam and His Circle*, which I have augmented with additional material that was not printed in the book, and more about their work in Arthur Bolton's, *The Architecture of Robert and James Adam*, which though published in 1922, has yet to be superseded. Howard Colvin's *Biographical Dictionary of British Architects*, has given a succinct account of all the brothers' careers, that is those of John, Robert, and James, and their father William Adam, as well as their architecture.

I

Drawing in Italy

THE EXPERIENCE OF the Adam brothers in Italy was one of intense intellectual development. The attainments of their Scottish education and the particular twist given to it by the family circle around William Adam, meant that the brothers were equipped to practise architecture in Scotland and to pursue a national career there, just like their father. To attain greater things needed a break with tradition and travel abroad – the longer, the better. For anybody interested in extending their understanding of the visual arts, in the eighteenth century, this meant almost certainly Italy. Such a decision first by Robert and then James was difficult but hardly surprising. More extraordinary, was its apparent lack of planning. Apart from setting Rome as a goal, little was prepared and much left to chance. Robert Adam's instruction in Rome by Clérisseau, Dewez, Lallemand and Piranesi, and his association with the various drawing academies there, were developments rather than strategies. For his brother James Adam, it was easier for he followed the footsteps. There can be little doubt that later on both of them were aware of the risks they had run. Robert Adam described such a hit or miss attitude with, 'I imagined that it would be sufficient for me to enlarge my ideas, to pick up a set of new thoughts which, with some little instruction in drawing, I imagined would be sufficient to make one who had seen so much carry all before him in a narrow country.'[1]

Though the two brothers may have been unclear about the means to the end, that end itself was never in much doubt. It was to have an understanding of classical architecture at first hand and an ability to effectively express it pictorially. This was the bedrock of the Adam style. Under the twin forces of Piranesi and Clérisseau, he studied both architecture and its delineation simultaneously and slowly evolved a drawing style that was both explanatory and evocative. It was an interpretation that he was later to express as the difference between the architectonic and the picturesque. Such a point of view,

[1] John Fleming, *Robert Adam and his Circle* (London, 1962), p. 168.

was expanded in the essay James Adam wrote in Rome, in 1762, and later in the prefaces he wrote for *The Works*, where words were matched to images. All of this was a slow business. The Roman years brought to the surface ideas that had been tentatively formed a decade earlier, reading and drawing in their father's library at Blair Adam. It was there that the sympathy for the classical past of Italy and imperial Rome was turned into something stronger than nostalgia and more positive than a taste for ruins.

The Blair Adam library was a conventional eighteenth-century one with a strong professional bias.[2] This slant was apparent in the good collection of architectural books acquired by William Adam before his death in 1748, and less obviously in the various topographic and landscape prints. Such books were more than evenly balanced by the conventional histories, some literature and the familiar classical authors. More of the schoolroom was apparent in works like Felton's, *Dissertation on reading the Classics and forming a just style*, of 1718, and the various editions of the classics themselves – Terence, of 1701, Horace, of 1699, Catullus, of 1702, Virgil, of 1701.[3] Less dull and more appealing in its view of antiquity was a Franco–Italian publication like the *Images des heros et des grands hommes de l'Antiquité*, of 1731 which may well have encouraged in the Adam brothers a visual interpretation of classicism beyond the normal one. But the most direct insight into Italy and things Italian was given by history such as Guicciardini, *La historia d'Italia*, 1636; more classically by Rossini's *Antiquitatem Romanorum* of 1701; and geographically, by Alberti Bolognese, *Descrittione di tutta l'Italia e Isole*, 1596. The more modern guide was represented by the *Descrittione di Roma Antica e Moderna* of 1643.[4] Such a library offered an understanding of the past in political and social terms, as well as showing the continuity of the classical imagination from Horace and Virgil to contemporary literature. William Adam's architectural books however, presented a rather more fragmentary account of architectural history and an uneven one of the development of style. On shelves thirty-one to thirty-nine, stood most of the standard renaissance authorities – Serlio, Scamozzi, Alberti and an Italian edition of Vitruvius – but the interpretation of the renaissance was essentially a French one, not a surprising state of affairs in Francophile Scotland.[5] There was a good

2   There are two extant catalogues to the library at Blair Adam before its dispersal at Sotheby's in 1926, for the last see Blair Adam Muniments 3/509. The earlier is a manuscript shelf list of 1785, made when some of the collection was removed to William Adam's chambers (Robert Adam's nephew) in Lincoln's Inn Fields. For an account of the 1785 list, see, *Architectural Heritage II: William Adam* (Edinburgh, 1990), pp. 8–33. The second was a privately printed catalogue, *Blair-Adam Library* (London, 1883).
3   Blair Adam Muniments 81/125.
4   *Ibid*.
5   The Blair Adam Vitruvius, catalogued as 'wants the Title Page' was probably the Venetian edition of 1567; the Serlio, *Le premier livre d'architecture* was a Paris edition of 1545; the Scamozzi,

collection of sixteenth- and seventeenth-century authors such as de L'Orme, Le Muet, Du Cerceau, Freart, de Brosse and a theorist like Perrault. Of them all, Adam preferred Le Pautre, 'the best French architect I ever knew'. Though the existing 1785 catalogue listed some of their Italian equivalents, such as Bartoli, Montano and Guarini, they were a more esoteric taste and more likely to have belonged to the later and expanded library of John Adam, Robert and James' elder brother, and possibly acquired for him in Italy.[6] The same provenance probably holds good for the Ruggieri of 1758 and the indispensable plate book of the Roman palaces, Falda and Ferrerio, *Palazzi di Roma*, which were all at Blair Adam before 1785.[7]

Such a library presented the Adam brothers with a conservative view of Italian classicism, glossed by that of France. While the books on literature and history opened Italy to the susceptible imagination, the architectural authors with their heavy number of illustrations gave a practical underpinning to any such flights of fancy. The way in which ideas could be turned into drawings was catered for by a book like the English edition of Pozzo's *Perspective proper for Painters and Architects*, of 1707. This probably directed the first steps of Adam draughtsmanship which ran from copying and adapting a wide range of prints, such as the pencil drawing after Lairesse's *Histoire de Didon et Aeneas*, to some incomplete figure groups where the perspective guidelines were just visible in the working up process (figure 1).[8] On the architectural front, a group of drawings for a hot and cold water 'Baths' was perhaps the most elaborate exercise of this 1750s period and, as such, was housed in the library alongside the architectural greats (figure 2). This dispersed portfolio showed the standard the brothers had reached by this time.[9] It was, in this way, virtually a textbook exercise, rather like the theoretical schemes they were later to produce in

Dell'idea architettura universale, Venice, 1615. There were also English editions by Leoni, *The Architecture of Palladio*, 1715, and Alberti, 'Architecture in 10 books, Painting in 3 Books', of 1726.

[6] The Blair Adam copy of Bartoli *Picturae Antiquae* (1750) was duplicated in the Adam sale of 1818, lot 117. The Blair Adam Montano, one volume, undated, had its counterpart in Robert Adam's Montani manuscripts, lot 33 of the 1818 sale. The trade in books was a two-way one, however, and in 1755 Robert Adam had Kent's *Inigo Jones*, Campbell's *Vitruvius* and Lord Burlington's *Baths*, all sent to him in Rome (London, Guildhall MS 3070 f. 11).

[7] The 1785 catalogue listed a *Palazzi di Roma di Pietro Ferrerio*, together with *Il nuovo teatro di Roma* (1665) which reappear in the 1883 catalogue. James Adam in 1762 compiled his list of Roman palaces to be seen from a copy of Falda and Ferrerio, and possibly this was the copy that appeared in the 1818 Adam sale.

[8] Blair Adam Collection, 427 and 660. On a folded sheet (48) was a series of notes on colours and their use in composition, presumably of this time.

[9] The drawings were described as 'A Description of the several Plans, Elevations & Sections for a Cold & Hot Bath with proper references for the better explaining the whole Apparatus necessary thereto'. The surviving sheets are in the Blair Adam Collection, 429, 430/1–3, 435, 591. 592.

Figure 1   Robert Adam,
after Lairesse, *Histoire de
Didon at Aeneas*

Rome, which showed both the building and the heating apparatus as well as
sheets of text explaining how it all worked. The drawings were accurate and flat,
strongly influenced by the hard outlines of engravings, with the details of
heating pipes carefully and economically coloured as though in some illustrated
textbook. It was a clear and simple style that was typical of the Adam Office at
this time. The 'Baths' scheme was paralleled by a miscellaneous group of small
drawings, remarkable for their extreme neatness and precision, with an almost
miniature-like air. They were too strikingly free of any obvious prototype,
though in terms of style they were certainly old-fashioned and looked more to
the relaxed classicism of Mannerism than the new broom of Palladianism.
Whatever influence was cast by the modern designs found in Gibbs' *Architecture*
or in the three volumes of Campbell's *Vitruvius Britannicus* (both in the library),
it lay lightly on such buildings.[10] Much more typical were the vigorous schemes
rooted in French architecture, such as Robert Adam's neat pen and wash design
for an entrance pavilion inspired by his reading of Du Cerceau's plates of
Chambord or the Chateau de Madrid (figure 3).[11] They had, however, few
distinct Italian counterparts and none that could be clearly identified with a

[10]   1785 catalogue, shelf 35.
[11]   *Ibid.*, shelf 37: *Architecture de Jacques Androvet de Cerceau* (Paris, 1648), and *Batiments de France, Par
     J. Androvet de Cerceau* (Paris, 1607).

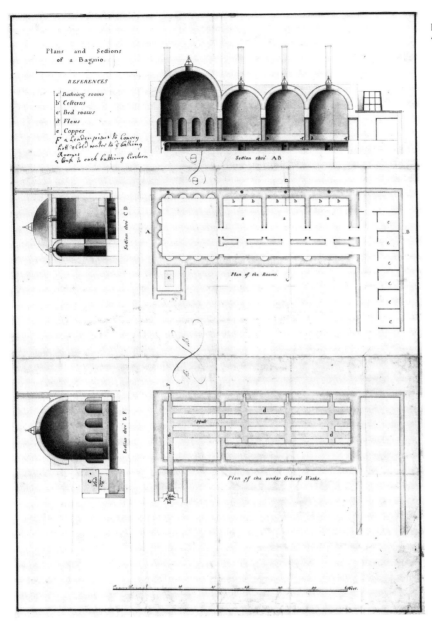

Figure 2   Robert Adam,
'Hot and Cold Baths'

popular and conventional work like Serlio's *Tutti libri di architettura* with its formidable range of hackneyed examples. Instead, such drawings revealed a wide imaginative response across a range of styles, recorded by a draughtsmanship capable of capturing detail crisply and decisively. Where landscape was involved, ink washes were replaced by rather bright colour. Altogether, they marked a critical period in Robert Adam's architectural education of which he

Figure 3 Robert Adam,
*Elevation for an Entrance
Pavilion*

was sufficiently aware to admit in 1755, that 'At London, I first felt the Change of Taste grow on me from what I contracted in Scotland.'[12]

The Adam understanding of the distinction that could be drawn between architectonic and picturesque was tentatively arrived at through the character of the Blair Adam library. Robert Adam's interest in the whole history of architecture and classicism in general was paralleled by an equal enthusiasm for landscape. The close proximity in the library of landscape prints and architectural engravings encouraged Adam to see the building's setting as the bridge between the picturesque and the more precise architectonic. The 1785 catalogue listed a folio of 'Landscapes etc by several Hands', and beside it a large drawing book and, for good measure, a portfolio of plans etc. of a house.[13] The landscape folio was identified in the 1883 catalogue as engravings after Gaspar Poussin and Claude, published by Knapton and Pond, in 1741–4.[14] How Robert and arguably James Adam turned these and similar prints into their picturesque scheme of things was simply by copying and studying them as closely as any architectural diagram. This much was quite explicit, in the laboured pen and ink landscape of Robert Adam, made in 1744 from a print after a landscape of Gaspar Dughet, where the devotion to detail overpowered the scene itself (figure 4).[15] This date and sort of overkill was apparent again in a group of equally undistinguished copies of rural prints after Marco Ricci,

[12] SRO GD 18/4764.

[13] 1785 catalogue, shelf 31.

[14] Blair Adam library, p. 56. For an account of this album see, Marie-Nicole Boisclair, *Gaspard Dughet* (Paris, 1986), p. 347, and Alain Roy, *Gérard de Lairesse* (Paris, 1992), p. 430.

[15] Soane Museum, AV LVI, f. 23. This drawing is very close in style and subject to ff. 6 and 14, the latter dated by Robert Adam as September, 1744.

Figure 4   Robert Adam,
Landscape after Gaspar Dughet

published in Venice in 1743.[16] In some of his drawings Adam seemed to have
followed the original accurately, as with his landscape of *Figures below a castle*,
while in others he allowed himself minor variations as in the sanitised copy of
Bandits attacking travellers (figure 6). In all of them, the subject was the
attraction for Adam and such landscapes with their conventional use of feudal
architecture, in mountainous or hilly scenery, were images that he returned to
frequently in his picturesque inventions of the 1780s. Like them too, Marco
Ricci remained a favourite and his paintings regularly appeared in the various
sales of the Adam collection from 1765 onwards.[17] The same sort of enthusiasm
for this type of landscape was shown in a drawing succinctly noted 'R. Adam
after S. Rosa', and in a copy after a Claude drawing that was probably later
acquired in Rome.[18] If nothing else, these rather dull variations began a
continuous pursuit of the art of landscape drawing, starting in the Blair Adam
library, quickening through the drawing academies of Rome until the wash and
watercolours of the 1770s and eighties where the picturesque and architectonic
were knitted together with unrivalled skill. That such a progress was a long and

[16]   The collection was published in Venice, in 1743, with prints by D. A. Fossati after Marco Ricci,
see L. Alpago-Novello, 'Gli incisori bellunesi: saggio storico-bibliografico', *Atti del Reale instituto
Veneto*, XCIX, 11, pp. 482–500. The surviving copies are in the Blair Adam Collection, 667,
669.

[17]   See pp. 72–8.

[18]   Soane Museum, AV LVI f. 31, dated 1751, and f. 159.

Figure 5   Robert Adam after
Marco Ricci, *Horseman in
Woodland*

Figure 6   D. F. Fossati after
Marco Ricci, *Bandits attacking
travellers*

difficult struggle was clear from Adam's acute limitations in the 1740s, where his
draughtsmanship with its unsubtle penmanship and the creaky construction of
his copies seemed to emphasise the stock motifs that he so arduously imitated.
He had much to learn even if allowance was made for a draughtsman in his late
teens.

In the eighteenth-century view of things, the picturesque was essentially a
landscape of the mind and better still the imagination, evoked as much by

painting as by the actual countryside. To reproduce the visual impact of such a
landscape, there had to be a fusion of mood and atmosphere with the more
bread and butter tradition of the topographic view. In Adam's case, prints can
be readily accepted as a substitute for the painting side in such an equation, and
his deep interest in topographic drawing was not hard to find. Once again, the
Blair Adam library and the family circle around it was the catalyst. The library
copy of Slezer's *Theatrum Scotiae*, of 1718, supplied a range of prints of sixteenth-
and seventeenth-century Scottish buildings, and more significantly, the
panoramas of small towns like Dunkeld and Musselburgh which it offered gave
an insight into the topographer's art.[19] How seriously the Adam family regarded
the latter was revealed in one at least of such panoramas, of the small seaside
town of Musselburgh, that they owned (figure 7).[20] The highly professional eye
of the Dutch topographer in which this townscape and its rural hinterland were
skilfully balanced, probably appealed to both Robert and James Adam and led
them to appreciate a more modern and sophisticated artist like Paul Sandby,
who had recently come to Scotland in the wake of the 1745 Rebellion. He
became part of the Adam circle through his employment in the Board of
Ordnance with which the brothers, like their father, were connected. Their
acquaintance with him continued until at least the publication of *The Ruins* in
1764. The pattern of artistic apprenticeship was the familiar one, with the Adam
brothers copying and imitating Sandby's views and so absorbing the formula he

Figure 7   John Slezer (?),
Panorama of Musselburgh

[19] John Slezer, *Theatrum Scotiae* (London, 1718); 1785 catalogue, shelf 33. For an account of Slezer
    and his draughtsmen see, James Holloway and Lindsay Errington, *The Discovery of Scotland*
    (Edinburgh, 1978), pp. 1–11.
[20] *Ibid.*, p. 11.

Figure 8   Robert Adam,
Elgin Cathedral

Figure 9   Paul Sandby,
Elgin Cathedral

had devised for turning the raw Scottish landscape into one acceptable to conventional eighteenth-century taste. There were a few drawings, such as that of Elgin Cathedral, where Robert Adam can be seen following behind Sandby – both pitching their views from the same spot on the river Lossie (figures 8 and 9). Though the balance of the two cathedral views remains the same, the essential immediacy and sparkle of the Sandby original has been lost, and one is a duller version of the other.

An additional Sandby pupil was Robert Adam's brother-in-law John Clerk.[21]

---

[21] For a succinct account of the Sandby–Clerk–Adam circle see, A. A. Tait, *The Landscape Garden in Scotland* (Edinburgh, 1980), pp. 110–18.

Figure 10   John Clerk,
Newark Castle

He was part of the same drawing circle at Blair Adam and shared the family enthusiasm for Scottish topography. Both Clerk and Robert Adam were diligent pupils who adapted and developed Sandby's lessons to their own rather different ends. Clerk remained throughout his life a dedicated topographer, fascinated by an architectural landscape which helped to lay bare the bones of Scottish history. He was far more able in that respect than either Adam or Sandby to pin down and control the antiquarian dimensions of the picturesque. His tiny bird's-eye views, and the later etchings made from them, of historic castles and distant townscapes were remarkable in the distillation of the character and mood of the scenery he drew with great sensitivity. It was in the use of colour that all three artists broke ranks. Sandby remained wedded to bright watercolour or gouache and a well-lit landscape, while Clerk settled for the more limited and duller tones of the ink wash as best suited to his miniature views. His delicate view of Newark Castle in Midlothian captured much of this small-scale subtlety and justified Adam's opinion that he was 'not exceeded even by any professional man I know'[22] (figure 10). Adam learnt from both. His technique of what he termed tinting was a mixture of toned down watercolour and ink wash, most effectively seen in his later picturesque views and architectural perspectives. Little of this subdued taste was apparent in his early, highly toned landscapes and architectural interiors where brilliance of design and

---

[22] SRO GD 248/3395/1. The best catalogue of Clerk's graphic work is offered by 'A Series of Etchings by John Clerk of Eldin', *Bannatyne Club* (Edinburgh, 1855) and 'Etchings chiefly views in Scotland', *Bannatyne Club* (Edinburgh, 1825). Adam's opinion of Clerk was given in a letter of 1788 to the Earl of Findlater.

colour were equated. In such a development, the guiding hand was not so much Sandby's but Clérisseau's, and the pace set by the drawings and landscape paintings Adam admired and collected in Italy.

In 1754, Robert Adam set out for Rome. His travelling companion was the aristocratic Charles Hope, son of one of his father's most faithful patrons, eighteen years his senior and successfully escaping from his wife.[23] He was at best a lukewarm grand tourist. It was not an easy relationship and one that did not last beyond the settling-in period in Rome. Adam's adopted and pretentious role of the scholar-connoisseur was probably too much for Hope. Free of him, Adam was able to shake loose from many of the conventions of the grand tourist, indulge his studies of the antique and renaissance to the full, and at a level smacking of ungentlemanly professionalism. He was at liberty to commission as well as collect drawings and so distinguish himself as the 'King of Artists'.[24] It was a reign that had begun casually enough when Adam met and became friendly with Claude Vernet in Marseille, en route for Italy, and through him received some sort of introduction and guidance to the artistic circles and various drawing academies in Rome.[25] Vernet, who had left the city in 1751, was well informed and had run a successful studio there among whose pupils had been Alexander Cozens. Adam probably knew what he was about, and his meeting with Clérisseau in Florence was perhaps not quite as accidental as he made out and may have been one of Vernet's suggestions.

The first public airing of Adam as the scholar-connoisseur was the trip to Naples of April, 1755, made with Clérisseau in attendance as his draughtsman and guide.[26] Apart from such a conspicuous display of scholarship and independence, this journey must have also brought home to Adam the gulf between his home-spun drawing style and that of his cosmopolitan companion. The drawing Adam made in January, 1755, of Porto Fino from the sea with its toy-town buildings and overworked penmanship showed how much Adam had to relearn (figure 11). In the light of this, the routine instruction of the Roman drawing academy was not only obligatory but essential if he was to benefit from Clérisseau's or anybody else's lessons. He was conscious too that an ability to draw, or appreciate drawing, was the further mark of the dilettante. How seriously Adam took such shortcomings was shown by the handful of figure drawings that have survived of his apprenticeship in the Roman drawing

[23] For Charles Hope see, Fleming, *Robert Adam*, pp. 340–1, and for Adam and Hope at the conclusion of their association, pp. 178–9.

[24] *Ibid.*, p. 161.

[25] *Ibid.*, p. 120.

[26] A summary of the journey and the drawing made during it is given in A. A. Tait, 'An Adam Volume in Sir John Soane's Museum', *Burlington Magazine*, 129 (1987), p. 743.

Sketch of the point & part of the Town of Porto Fino from the Bay

162

taken on the spot 18 January 1755

Figure 11 Robert Adam, 'Sketch of the point & part of the Town of Porto Fino'

schools.[27] He moved quickly and was associated possibly with that of Mengs or, more likely Batoni, by early 1755. Adam was introduced to the latter by either Clérisseau or his associate Pecheux, who had arrived in Rome in 1753. Pecheux seems to have acted as Adam's figure man, through whom the arrangements and lessons at the school were made, a programme devised and progress noted. He inspired confidence and Adam readily accepted him as a translator of the language of academe, offering his interpretation of the classical cast or life drawing as a sort of crib. A set of red chalk studies after the antique were acquired from him by Robert Adam at this time, and the surviving head showed the academic style taught and demanded in such a school (figure 12).[29] The organisation of such studios in Rome did not vary much and Batoni's was not greatly different from its rivals. It was open to all for a small fee, took place

[27] Such drawings as have survived are in the Blair Adam Collection, see National Register of Archives handlist (1976). A few appear in the salerooms from time to time, such as *Two Heads*, lot 93, Sotheby's (April, 1992). Some of these were probably copies of the 'Academy figures, some Heads, Hands & Feet' which Adam bought from Cipriani in May, 1755, on the understanding that they 'will do your business nicely'. (SRO GD 18/4764.)

[28] Fleming, *Robert Adam*, pp. 163–4.

[29] Several of these appeared in the Adam sale of 1818, along with similar 'Academy studies', by Lallemand and Clérisseau. (Arthur Bolton, *The Architecture of Robert and James Adam*, 2 vols., London, 1922, II, p. 331.)

Figure 12   Laurent Pecheux,
Classical head

roughly during the winter season and followed a traditional pattern of copying
from paintings, antique casts or drawing from the model.[30] Pupils followed
Batoni's drawing style with precise compositions in black or white chalk on blue
prepared paper or with red chalk on white, of which examples appeared in the
Adam auctions.[31] It was convenient too for Adam, being near Santa Trinità dei
Monti and so close to his rooms in the Casa Guarnieri. Though Adam studied
hard there and both Pecheux and Batoni were competent teachers, his work as
a figure artist never passed beyond the nearly competent. A drawing, likely to
have been his and from this period, of a youth praying, showed little technical
dexterity in the clumsy draughtsmanship of the clasped hands, shortcomings all
the more real when compared with Pecheux's *Head of an old man*, that Adam

[30] For an account of Batoni's academy and his drawing style see, Anthony Clark, *Pompeo Batoni*
(Oxford, 1985), pp. 36–9.
[31] Bolton, *Architecture*, II, p. 331.

Figure 13   Robert Adam, *Youth at prayer*   Figure 14   Laurent Pecheux, *Head of an old man*

possessed (figures 13 and 14). For all his and Pecheux's efforts, he had not come
far but perhaps far enough for his assumed part as connoisseur and architect. In
the latter role, excellence in figure drawing was hardly essential, only moder-
ately useful and certainly not as vital a talent as an ability to depict and conceive
landscape. For help here, Adam turned again through Clérisseau, to Jean-
Baptiste Lallemand, his anonymous 'good master' of landscape.

Lallemand's association with Adam was a shadowy one which Adam was
typically keen to keep that way. He did little to promote his career when he
turned up in London in 1773, though this did not discourage him from
conscientiously collecting his work, in the same way as he did that of Pecheux.[32]
Adam was sympathetic and even envious of the nostalgic landscape he evoked
in his finished views of Tivoli, the Forum, or the Ponte Molle, different from
the stronger architectural interpretations of much the same spots offered by

32 Adam paid little attention to either Clérisseau, who appeared in London in 1771, or Lallemand
who exhibited at the Society of Artists in 1773. See, Thomas McCormick, *Charles-Louis
Clérisseau and the Genesis of Neo-Classicism* (London, 1990), pp. 147–61, and Algernon Graves, *The
Society of Artists of Great Britain* (London, 1907), pp. 58, 141. For an account of Lallemand's
Roman career see, Andrea Busiri Vici, 'Opere Romane di Jean-Baptiste Lallemand', *L'Urbe* 5
(Rome, 1977), pp. 1–5; and Oliver Michel, 'Recherches sur Jean-Baptiste Lallemand à Rome',
Piranèse et les Français: Academie de France à Rome (Rome, 1978), pp. 333–5.

Figure 15 Jean Baptiste
Lallemand, *Roman garden*

Clérisseau. He had little interest, too, in the bright colours of Clérisseau's gouaches which made his pencil and chalk drawings seem all the more casual and low key. Lallemand was at his best where the topographic element was of lesser importance, in what the Adam sale catalogue of 1818 referred to as 'Italian Garden scenery' (figure 15).[33] In these works, with their crumbling terraces and overgrown gardens, filled with the derictus of antiquity, he approached the atmospheric drawings of his Roman contemporaries Hubert Robert and Fragonard, though he never matched their fluent draughtsmanship or evocation of grander themes. Possibly such creative limitations made it the easier for Adam to understand him and interpret his work with the considerable ease shown in his wash of a *Landscape with antique fragments* of the late 1750s, which has moved little from Lallemand's grand tour setpiece of the Villa Ludovisi gardens (figures 16 and 17). It was a path that Adam continued along with increasing confidence and this allowed him later, and probably in the 1780s, to convert a straightforward topographic view of the Tomba del Somaro in the Pignetta Sacchetti into an atmospheric watercolour for some garden monument (figure 18, plate 1). More typical but less attractive was Robert Adam's sketchbook of antique fragments in a landscaped park, directed by Lallemand whose hand, literally in some instances, lay across it.[34] Such a collaboration was to be expected, and the grouping together of works by Adam

[33] Bolton, *Architecture*, II, p. 331.

[34] New York, Pierpont Morgan Library, Landscape Album. The title is a hand similar to that of the Adam volumes in the Soane reads, 'Contents of this Volume 39 Designs on Tinted paper by R. Adam'.

Figure 16   Jean Baptiste Lallemand, *View of the Palazzino in the Villa Ludovisi, Rome*

Figure 17   Robert Adam, *Landscape with antique fragments*

and Lallemand, as a lot in an Adam sale, showed the remarkable affinity between teacher and pupil.[35]

Lallemand was in Rome from 1747 until around 1761, and so his connection was with Robert rather than James Adam. The sheets in this surviving sketchbook, probably of 1757 and now in the Pierpont Morgan Library, were all grey

[35] In the 1818 sale lot 32 referred to 'Elegant drawings in India Ink by L'Alma, of Italian Garden scenery with old drawings on the back', and lot 35 consisted of one Adam drawing and three by Lallemand. (Bolton, *Architecture*, II, p. 331.)

Figure 18 Robert Adam, *Garden Monument* watercolour after the Tomba del Somaro, Rome

washed, characteristic of Lallemand's taste for working on coloured paper. The drawings themselves were an odd lot. Few were finished and several little more than pencil outlines. The sketchbook was not an account of any topographic tour in the style of those of Clérisseau, and the subjects themselves range widely

Figure 19   Robert Adam,
Classical buildings in a landscape

– even wildly – from landscape to Roman sculpture.[36] It seems almost certain to have been a studio rather than a *plein air* production and the landscape sketches themselves have a heavily contrived air. One of the more atmospheric was a landscape with a waterfall amongst classical ruins where Adam and Lallemand's enthusiasms were evenly matched in this study of evocative dereliction (figure 19). The sketchbook can perhaps be best explained as a sort of continuous studio lesson between Adam and his landscape instructor, never finished and later used for odds and ends. The drawings that were completed did not show any significant steps in Adam's understanding of picturesque composition and still lack the subtle integration of architecture with landscape that he had so admired, and copied, in Marco Ricci's prints. It is possible, too, that they were some sort of dummy run for his suggested collection of landscape scenes of the temple and cascade variety, mentioned in a letter to his brother John in 1756.[37] In his mind also at this time was a similar book on landscape architecture, though it was to be different in showing 'executed' rather than proposed designs with each plate dedicated to its owner.[38] In this respect, it was

[36] Several sheets were unprepared, ff. 35, 36, and f. 39 had been greyed but unused; f. 2 was a drawing of a piece of classical sculpture while f. 34 was a pencil design for an arabesque panel.

[37] Fleming, *Robert Adam*, p. 363.

[38] *Ibid.*

a forerunner for Adam's picturesque panoramas of about 1782, of which only that of Oxenfoord was apparently published (figure 105).

In 1755, Adam in Rome divided taste into what he termed picturesque and architectonic, perhaps his variation on the traditional painting contrast between Rubensisme and Poussinisme. Architectonic presumably meant for him a narrow and rather rigid way of visualising architecture which he contrasted with his own broad and sentimental attitude of the picturesque. While Clérisseau, Piranesi and Lallemand encouraged such a taste which mixed buildings and landscape in a pictorial fashion, the more circumspect view of building and architectural design was taught by the architect draughtsman Laurent-Benoît Dewez.[39] In Adam's way of thinking, he was the master of the architectonic, a perhaps dull but necessary mentor who brought to earth Adam's flights of picturesque fancy. To him fell the thankless task of instruction in the prosaic business of casting plans and sections and making accurate elevations. It proved a successful, perhaps necessary, arrangement, for Dewez returned with Adam to London in 1757, having served his time on both the abortive Desgodetz and Spalatro recording enterprises. He had joined Adam in Rome by 1756, and was somewhat condescendingly described as 'the plan man and line drawer'.[40] Possibly Adam was a little apprehensive of a virtual employee of much the same age, who had a greater mastery of the conventional skills of an architect and already some standing in the profession. On Dewez's part, there can only have been mounting exasperation at having to play second fiddle for so long to so inconsiderate a pupil. As an architect and possible pupil of Vanvitelli, there was a limit to his capacity to copy and work up Adam's schemes without recognition and this no doubt came to a head with his flight from London and Adam, in 1759.[41] If his three bay portico for the abbey of Gembloux, built after his return to Belgium in 1762, is compared with its rougher Adam prototype at Shardeloes, begun when Dewez was still the principal assistant in the Adam office, his frustration was certainly understandable (figures 20 and 21).[42]

A surviving group of Dewez's drawings in Brussels belonged to the period of

---

[39] For Dewez's Roman drawings see, Simone Ansiaux, 'Les Dessins d'Italie de Laurent-Benoît Dewez', *Bulletin de l'Institut Historque Belge de Rome* (1952), pp 1–15; and more generally, H. Gerson and E. H. ter Kuile, *Art and Architecture in Belgium, 1600–1800* (Harmondsworth, 1960), p. 33.

[40] Fleming, *Robert Adam*, p. 216.

[41] His association with Vanvitelli is historical rather than documentary, Ansiaux, 'Les Dessins d'Italie', p. 9. His name for instance, does not appear in M. R. Caroselli, *La Regia di Caserta, Lavori costo effetti della Constuzione* (Milan, 1968), pp. 35–47.

[42] The architectural drawings for Shardeloes are in Soane Museum, AV XXXI, ff. 97–109, The draughtsmanship, especially of f. 101, was in the simple clear style of the Scottish office. For Gembloux see, Gerson and ter Kuile, *Art and Architecture*, p. 33.

Figure 20   Robert Adam, *Entrance portico at Shardloes*   Figure 21   Laurent-Benoît Dewez, *Entrance portico at Gembloux Abbey*

the 1750s.[43] Some of them overlapped with a dismembered Adam sketchbook, or books, in the Soane Museum of much the same time.[44] Almost all had a strongly pedagogic character as did what has remained of Dewez's architectural archive, antique and modern. His surviving pencil sketches of the ever popular maritime theatre of the Villa Adriana at Tivoli taught a clarity and competence essential for a successful survey of any antique monument, as Adam perhaps ruefully recalled when bringing *The Ruins* to the press.[45] Rather more interesting, and aesthetically pleasing, was the plan for the Roman baroque church of Santa Maria in Portico di Campitelli where Dewez's sophisticated technique matched the elaborate contemporary style associated with the competition drawings of the Roman Concorso Clementino.[46] The usefulness to

[43] Ansiaux, 'Les Dessins d'Italie', pp. 4–15.
[44] Soane Museum, AV IX. This is divided into five sections, of which the first section is drawings before 1758, executed whilst abroad, and the rest after the return to London. The drawings are haphazardly arranged and came originally from several sketchbooks of different sizes, and there is no absolute division between the various sections, though f. 149, a post-1758 design, was clearly on a letter dated in London, 25 January 1758.
[45] Ansiaux, 'Les Dessins d'Italie', p. 6, no. 52.
[46] *Ibid.*, p. 8, no. 37.

Figure 22   Laurent-Benoît
Dewez, *Domed pavilion with
wings*

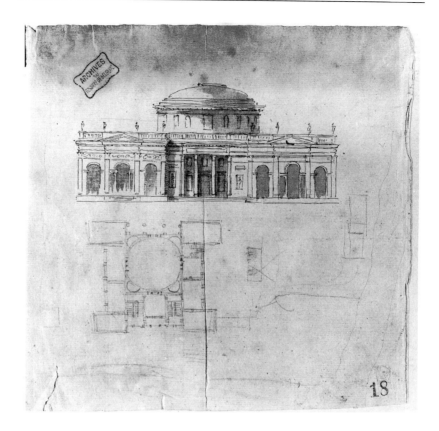

Adam of these and similar exercises was self-evident, they provided him with a
range of practical drawing styles, clear, economical and elegant, but apart from
that they reveal little of Dewez's influence on any of the more critical areas of
Adam's architecture. It is hard to see in the Soane sketches any clear advance
in Adam's handling of space or ease and sensitivity in planning. They tend to
confirm Dewez's position at this stage as Adam's 'plan man'.

Dewez's remaining sketch designs can suggest a different interpretation and
hint at the two men working in an ambiguous and ill-defined collaboration.
Adam's scaled plan for a villa with a circular hall was almost identical to a copy
drawing found in the Dewez collection in Brussels.[47] Taken perhaps the other
way around, Dewez's plan and elevation for a domed pavilion with wings can
be compared with much the same scheme in the dismembered Soane sketchbook (figure 22).[48] These and others make reasonably clear the nature of the
learning process where Adam was the pupil, absorbing and refining the shorthand of classical composition. A frequent exercise set by Dewez was the villa

[47] Soane Museum, AV IX, f. 11, 'Les Dessins d'Italie', no. 10.
[48] 'Les Dessins d'Italie', p. 15, no. 18 is a version of AV IX, f. 159 (elevation) and ff. 46, 48 (plans).

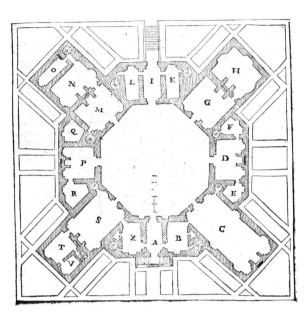

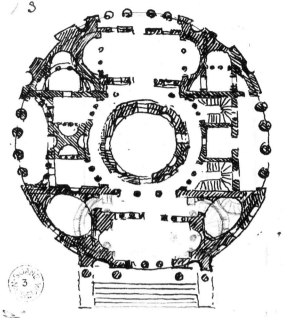

Figure 23   Sebastiano Serlio, *Tutte l'opere d'architettura*   Figure 24   Robert Adam, *Theoretical scheme for a circular building*

with a central hall, an appropriate textbook project derived from book VII of Serlio's *Architettura*, which Adam drew repeatedly in both pencil and ink, and composed a series of variations, some which certainly rubbed off in the very early designs for Lansdowne House (figures 23 and 24).[49] A few of these may have been in Dewez's hand, and one rather naively showed him practising his English phonetically, – 'Cela suffit. That is enough. That is enuff'.[50] The success of his instruction was clear enough and through it Adam learnt to cast plans 'like peas from my knife'. These and especially his minute villa schemes, signposted the distance Adam had smoothly travelled from the Blair Adam designs almost a decade ago. They matched the similar lengths he had completed alongside Pecheux and Lallemand. But in all of this, the directing hand was that of Clérisseau who never lost control of his French associates. During his troubles with James Adam in 1761, he made clear to the Adam draughtsman, George Richardson, that Robert Adam had been 'wholly directed by me in everything, he never did one thing without taking my advice'.[51]

[49]   Sebastiano Serlio, *Tutte L'Opere d'Architettura* (Venice, 1584) book VII, pp. 27–31; and Soane Museum, AV IX, ff. 4, 5 with variations on ff. 2, 3, 16, 23, 25, 26. For the early schemes for Lansdowne House of *c.* 1764, see Bolton, *Architecture*, II, p. 2.

[50]   Soane Museum, AV IX, f. 17.

[51]   Fleming, *Robert Adam*, p. 286.

With such associates, Adam had channelled the imagination of his Sandby days into more conventional academic forms. The effect was to lay a modern and fashionable education on top of one idiosyncratically and haphazardly picked up from the prints and books in William Adam's library. Though Robert Adam may have believed in serendipity, Clérisseau did not. For him, academic rigour lay at the heart of artistic success. However, the smoothness and logic of this relearning process was perhaps deliberately disturbed by the inclusion of Piranesi in this small circle. He may have appealed to Adam as a sort of catalyst whose inconsistency and unconventionality provided the kind of stimulus that he needed from time to time. More than that, there was in Adam an intellectual void, or at least uncertainty about architectural theory that Piranesi filled if not by words, then certainly by example. Piranesi's respect at this time – the 1750s – for the doctrines of utilitarianism and rigorism, culled from his fellow Venetian Carlo Lodoli, struck a common chord in Adam's deeply practical nature where he expected a drawing to work for its living and bring in a commission. Both Robert and James Adam's contact with Lodoli's rigorist theories was through his apologist Algarotti, who James Adam had met in Bologna in 1760 and Robert in Rome during 1757.[52] Apart from this encounter Adam was left to absorb and interpret such opinions as best he could through Piranesi's prints and drawings. Hidden behind Robert Adam's respect for the classical iconoclast, were his less defined and more general ideas which supported such a broad view of architecture and its history. His constant interest in the sympathetic mixture of the gothic and classical styles, came as much from Piranesi as from a reading of the French exponent of the same view, the Abbé Laugier, whose *Essai sur l'architecture*, of 1753 was already a force in the French Academy at the Palazzo Mancini.[53] Laugier's attitude to a stylistic *laissez-faire* which accepted the merits of both styles and even encouraged their deliberate mixture as had been apparent in the contemporary rebuilding, in 1756, of the Parisian church of St Germain l'Auxerrois. It could equally well have been found in contemporary Rome, and this was a lesson well understood by Adam, at least visually. All of this was underpinned for him and others by a seminal work like Debos, *Réflexions critiques sur la poésie et sur la peinture* which identified a moral sixth sense of good taste that protected the educated eye.[54] Whether the Adam brothers borrowed rather than owned such books was not

[52] *Ibid.*, p. 234. According to James Adam's journal, he met Algarotti in Bologna in November, 1762 (*Library of The Fine Arts* 3 vols. (London, 1831), II, p. 172). For the relationship between Lodoli and his posthumous biographer Francesco Algarotti see, Joseph Rykwert, *The First Moderns* (London, 1980), pp. 288–399.

[53] Wolfgang Herrmann, *Laugier and Eighteenth Century French Theory* (London, 1962), pp. 191–6.

[54] *Ibid.*, p. 39.

made clear from their library, though John Adam had Laugier at Blair Adam and Robert Adam took the *Philosophical Transactions* until 1780. Possibly some more were included in the 'on Painting' lot disposed of during the 1821 auction.[55]

Robert Adam had met Piranesi in 1755 and by the following year their relationship had developed sufficiently for Adam to be singled out as one of Piranesi's leading patrons. Their friendship was cemented by the partial dedication to him in 1756, of volume II of the *Antichità Romane*. They remained friends until Adam's departure from Rome the next year. It was during this time that Adam acquired the Piranesi drawings, now in the Soane Museum, and made several drawing expeditions with him and others around Rome. During such trips, it was unlikely that the volatile Piranesi gave Adam anything more than the most cursory of instruction and the slightest encouragement. His influence was instead on Adam's susceptible, picturesque imagination where its hold was gradual and oblique. In Piranesi's view of things, the remains of antique Rome were a snare which deceived the superficial sightseer and blinded him to the true role of classical architecture. Into this category he probably cast both Adam and Clérisseau, for whose salvation he was prepared to struggle if the price was right. The fragments of Rome were, for Piranesi, a means to understanding an infinitely greater and more complex problem which he attempted to explain through his prints. This was a large part of the message of his *Antichità Romane* and he continued in more polemical fashion four years later with the *Della magnificenza ed architettura de' Romani*, of 1761, in which he emphasised the practical, if not utilitarian, aspects of so much of Roman civil architecture. In much of this, he was effectively illustrating the rigorist theories of Lodoli and Algarotti.[56] If the reason and purpose of the familiar Arch of Constantine or the Colosseum were easily grasped by Piranesi's readers, that of an overbuilt and decayed site like the Campus Martius was not. This sort of intellectual archaeology was not entirely appreciated by Adam for whom it perhaps smacked too much of the tendentious, Scottish antiquarianism of his father's patron Sir John Clerk.

Such an apparent lack of understanding on Adam's part was very clearly shown in the drawings he made with Piranesi around Castel Gandolfo and the Lago del Albano. They show the tower at the head of the lake from two slightly different standpoints but neither of Adam's drawings repeated exactly the view which Piranesi selected for his print, published in the *Emissario del Lago Albano*,

---

[55] Bolton, *Architecture*, II, p. 334: and *Sale Catalogues of Libraries of Eminent Persons*, ed. D. J. Watkin (London, 1972), p. 153.

[56] Rykwert, *First Moderns*, pp. 315–17, 389.

Figure 25   G. B. Piranesi,
*Dimostrazioni e Disegno
dell'Emissario del Lago Albano*

of 1762 (figures 26 and 27).[57] All of the illustrations made a forceful contrast between the present simple and rather primitive usage of the site as a peasant washing place, and the sophisticated and complicated piece of hydraulic engineering buried below ground and threatened by a relentless, engulfing nature. In such a fashion, antique standards were established and decline emphasised with typical Piranesian irony. This element of enquiry and pointed criticism, coupled with a curiosity about past and present, was absent from Adam's two sketches where the empty foregrounds and dull backgrounds had little point to make about the human condition (figure 26).[58] But where he could only see a dreary landscape around a tower, Piranesi supplied his view with a road and picturesque cottages stretching into the distance and so emphasised the height, stability, and durability of the tower (figure 27). Piranesi's composition had too a liveliness and sense of drama that Adam failed to match. His drawing of a mule loaded with water-carriers seemed innocuous compared with Piranesi's disturbing ruffians and threatening washerwomen.

Adam's insensitivity to the moral significance of Piranesi's drawings and prints, put him in the good company of Lallemand and Clérisseau, who offered a largely conventional interpretation of the topographic view. The figures that

[57] For an account of the development of Piranesi's interest in the Lago del Albano from the Campus Martius, with its map dedicated to Adam, see Jonathan Scott, *Piranesi* (London, 1975), pp. 165–70.
[58] Rykwert, *First Moderns*, p. 370.

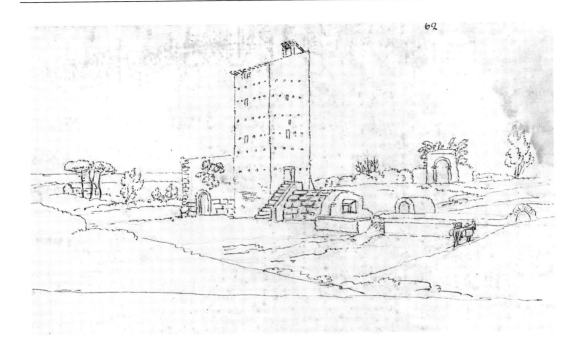

62

Figure 26 Robert Adam,
*The Jesuit's garden at Castel
Gandolfo*

Adam, or for that matter Clérisseau employed, were the traditional subordinate ones of *staffage*.

Lively and busy in the urban views, languorous and rustic in the landscape ones, such figures lack the jarring quizzical air of Piranesi's people who disturb rather than extend the artist's soothing mood. In the view of the canal entrance at the Lago del Albano, Piranesi's figures are a strange group who seem forcibly contrasted with the respectable antiquarian with hat and cane – the essential elements of gentility. On the right hand of the same print, a hopeless figure slumps half asleep, another lights a fire, a third gesticulates at the massive wall and, on the left, a man points upwards to a staring youth (figure 25). Such decayed and ragged humans matched the ruined structure and none induced the atmosphere of contentment or melancholy so earnestly sought by the conventional *vedutisti*.

Closer to Adam's imaginative limitations was Clérisseau, whose instruction was vital if any effective headway was to be made. While Piranesi had perhaps the congenial role of upsetting Adam's visual apple-cart, Clérisseau's was to set it straight again on academic tracks. Though a difficult character, Clérisseau was a stylish and inventive drawing master, concerned with presentation rather than theory and intent on making Adam as excellent an artist as his recent pupil and Adam's future rival, William Chambers.[59] He too was part of the triumvirate

[59] John Harris, *Sir William Chambers* (London, 1970), pp. 23–4.

31

Figure 27 G. B. Piranesi,
*Dimostrazioni e Disegno
dell'Emissario del Lago Albano*

Figure 28 C. L. Clérisseau,
*Entrance to the tunnel at Castel
Gandolfo*

that assembled at the Lago del Albano, and a surviving drawing by him was
made from virtually the same spot as Adam's (figure 28).[60] Both were straightforward topographic accounts without figures and each boldly exploited the
suckering tree on the right of the scene. Invention and interpretation were

[60] See, A. A. Tait, 'Reading the Ruins, Robert Adam and Piranesi in Rome', *Design and Practice in
British Architecture*, ed. John Newman (London, 1984), pp. 524–8.

Figure 29   Robert Adam,
Design for a Roman Ruin

firmly controlled and the two artists fail to see far beyond their topographic noses. Piranesi's principal concern in his plate had been to show the vastness and monumentality of Roman utilitarian architecture by exaggerating the masonry of the arch and flanking walls (figure 25). It was not an insight that either Adam or Clérisseau ostensibly shared, they more or less recorded what they saw. But it would be wrong to assume that Adam was deaf to any response to ruined antiquity other than a topographic one, or insensitive to any moral interpretations. His two pen sketches for the side rooms of a domed, antique pavilion were annotated by him in French – so presumably made in Rome with Clérisseau and Dewez at his shoulder. They emphasised Adam's typically graphic exploration of the ways in which the past might be interpreted.[61] The watercolour of the domed hall showed an artist at work recording the antique fragments, presumably discovered by his workmen (figure 29). The two side rooms were decorated in conflicting styles, one completely tricked out with antique fragments, the other fitted up as a small chapel in contemporary style. The Janus-like pavilion presented, as it were, the options open to the architect

---

[61]   McCormick, *Clérisseau*, pp. 111–12, and for a more critical account, Alistair Rowan, *Catalogue of Architectural Drawings in the Victoria and Albert Museum: Robert Adam* (London, 1988), pp. 33, 53.

Figure 30 Robert Adam,
*View of the interior of Santa
Maria degli Angeli*

concerned with the past. He could remodel in the antiquarian style of the Villa
Albani or Clérisseau's ruined room at Santa Trinità dei Monti, or the Rock
Room at Kedleston for that matter, or simply fling past and present together as
Vanvitelli had done at Santa Maria degli Angeli and create a modern space, as
Adam prosaically recorded (figure 30).[62] While these drawings hardly reflected
any acute dilemma for Adam, they show a sensitivity to the various moods a ruin
could evoke and the ways through which they might be satisfied. They were
alternatives to Piranesi's solution at the Lago del Albano and no doubt were in
line with Clérisseau's compartmentalised thinking.

The drawings that Robert, and later James Adam made with Clérisseau, were
almost exclusively of antiquity or its interpretation during the renaissance.
While this may have turned the Adam heads in a particular direction, it did not
entirely blind them to the work of their contemporaries who were in a sense
future rivals. Adam organised, presumably through Dewez 'to do the fountains,
the buildings, the statues' of Rome which were to be later essential source
material for the Adam office as Pecheux's similar survey had been for Chambers,
in 1753.[63] The three surviving drawings of Salvi's newly completed Trevi
Fountain, the remains of the 160 drawings that Soane bought as 'A Scrapbook'

[62] For the Kedleston Rock Room see, Leslie Harris, *Robert Adam and Kedleston* (London, 1987),
p. 84, no. 71.
[63] Fleming, *Robert Adam*, p. 152, for Pecheux and Chambers see, Harris, *Sir William Chambers*,
p. 24, and John Pinto, *The Trevi Fountain* (New Haven, 1986), p. 354.

Figure 31 Circle of Laurent
Pecheux, *Trevi Fountain,
Rome*

in the 1818 sale, showed the modern character of this ambitious collection
(figure 31).[64] Salvi's architecture was admired by Adam as among the 'good
buildings' of Rome, and all three Trevi drawings of chalk on blue paper,
emphasised and exaggerated the sculpture of the fountain at the expense of the
architecture.[65] In this, they were probably superior to what is known of the
drawings Pecheux supplied to Chambers, and they must have appealed more to
Robert Adam's picturesque than architectonic sense. Adam was in this way,
sizing up his competitors by stealth, but apart from this survey contemporary
architecture along with contemporary architects were rarely discussed in any
greater depth than the brothers' remarks on Caserta. Though Dewez with his
possible connections with Vanvitelli provided links with other Roman offices
which Adam may well have exploited, little was said of them. Adam's drawings
of the interior of Santa Maria degli Angeli, made in May, 1755, revealingly
showed as much interest in its 'being fitted up by an Italian Architect Vanvitelli',
as enthusiasm for the antique Baths of Diocletian.[66] The reason for such a
restricted view of the past was a simple one. To the brothers, the antique was

[64] Soane Museum, AV LVI, ff. 55–7; and Watkin, *Sale Catalogues*, p. 173.
[65] Fleming, *Robert Adam*, p. 359.   [66] SRO GD 18/4775.

the source for all later styles and, like all aspiring neoclassicists, they were interested in returning to the heart of architecture and so constructing their own uncorrupted version of antiquity. Nothing perhaps provided a better insight into such a deliberately shuttered view than Robert Adam's drawings at Ancona, where the Arch of Trajan was laboriously recorded but its contemporary neighbour, Vanvitelli's Arco Clementino, was neglected, possibly at Clérisseau's jealous suggestion (figure 32). The shortcut to such knowledge was the renaissance. It provided a reliable guide both to the past and its interpretation and it was this line of thought that had encouraged Robert Adam's interest in expanding and republishing Desgodetz's *Edifices antiques de Rome*, which last appeared in 1695.[67] It was equally clear that the renaissance appealed to the brothers more as a means than as an end in itself, a position unchanged from their days reading in the library at Blair Adam. While the brothers were prepared to see the greatest merit in the Ligorio drawings in the Albani collection and Robert was prepared to copy Peruzzi and Raphael, the same view did not extend to renaissance architecture in general. At Bramante's San Pietro in Montorio, James Adam was amazed that 'he could produce nothing more tolerable, nothing more correct, nothing more ingenious than this', and the same scorn was directed at the Cancellaria as 'lacking genius, taste and elegance'.[68]

The Adam brothers assumed in their attitude to the renaissance the curious position of self-conceived rivals, pitting themselves against the traditional interpretation of the antique.[69] Consequently, they saw Brunelleschi or Palladio in much the same light as an obvious architectural competitor such as Robert Mylne or William Chambers. The errors that Robert Adam detected in Palladio's drawings for the reconstruction of the 'Baths', published in 1730 as *Fabbriche antiche disegnate da Andrea Palladio*, encouraged a dismissive attitude to Palladio and led him to question the accuracy of the renaissance as a reliable recorder of classical architecture.[70] It became easy for the brothers to delude themselves into thinking that they alone possessed a deep insight into the antique and had the knowledge necessary to correct the errors of renaissance draughtsmen. But such an arrogant stance was more a public one, which did not stand in the way of their serious study of the renaissance or their need to

[67] Fleming, *Robert Adam*, p. 170.
[68] SRO GD 18/4454, f. 45.
[69] The best account of the brothers' attitude to renaissance architecture – certainly James Adam's – was given in the incomplete history of architecture, of 1762. (SRO GD 18/4954, ff. 27–57.) It ranged from Brunelleschi to Michelangelo and relied heavily on Baldinucci *Notie de' professori del disegno* (Florence, 1681) and for buildings selected from Ferrerio and Falda's *Palazzi di Roma* (Rome, 1726). The Falda may be that which appeared in the Adam sale of 1818 as lot 57.
[70] Fleming, *Robert Adam*, p. 218.

Figure 32   Robert Adam,
Roman Arch at Ancona

borrow directly from it, from time to time. The enormous variety found there appealed to them as much as the inventive classicism of the antique. It was the style they favoured for the octagon contemplated for the bottom of their garden at Lower Grosvenor Street, as perhaps an appropriately flexible background for their collection of antique fragments and sculpture (figures 67 and 68). It remained too the prime source for much of their relief decoration and grotesque work, certainly until the early 1770s. The attempt by Robert Adam then to popularise a renaissance *palazzo* style as part of his picturesque vocabulary marked the high-water mark of his interest and his confidence in a renaissance as distinct from an antique revival (figure 141).[71]

Like all pupils, the two Adam brothers felt the need to bring their period of study to some sort of formal conclusion. Such an ending would clearly demonstrate progress made, abilities attained, techniques explored, and professional standing established. For Dewez and Clérisseau, brought up in the world of competition and prizes, the most satisfactory route to all of this was through the architectural competition with its emphasis on the grand manner and paper solutions. The form this took in Rome, was the Concorso Clementino where prizes were awarded as much on the ability to draw convincingly and compose coherently and impressively as anything else. The practical considerations of building were not something with which the theoretical *concorso* greatly

[71] See pp. 162–5.

37

concerned itself. For Robert and James Adam, such a competition or its equivalent could encourage them to produce a series of fashionable drawings that would catch and dazzle the eye and so make a suitable exit from Rome. Better still, such designs should overwhelm critical taste later on in London and set fresh and rigorous standards for their pupils and rivals.

2

The *concorso* style

AN UNDERSTANDING OF the Italian architectural drawing was at the root of the brothers' time in Italy. As connoisseurs and collectors, they had developed a sharp eye for invention and quality, as well as a wide knowledge of the history of drawing. From such a standpoint, Robert Adam at least was prepared to look beyond the drawing sheet and see a whole schema of architecture. Such an imaginative response focused his attention on the theoretical drawing of the sort to which he had been introduced by Dewez and Clérisseau, and which was symbolised by the Roman Concorso Clementino. Though the Adam plans for Lisbon and the Westminster Parliament were intended as ambitious proposals rather than the paper projects of the Italian competitions, they belonged intellectually at least to this way of thinking. Furthermore, all such drawings had an obviously public face which drew equal attention to author and architecture, as the Adam brothers well understood. It was for them a statement about what had been absorbed in Rome, their easy command of classicism, and skill in composing and drawing in the grand manner of the Italian academies.

The final statement about a prolonged period of architectural study in Rome or elsewhere in Italy, was the production of a large, theoretical scheme for usually some public building.[1] The subject was frequently chosen as much as a means for a virtuoso display of draughtsmanship as of design. The simple vehicles for this were the *concorsi* of the various Italian academies, of which those of Rome and Bologna were the most prestigious. The former was run by the Accademia di San Luca, under papal patronage.[2] Logically enough, the majority of the subjects set were for religious buildings of some sort, but apart from that it showed a fondness for simple geometric shapes and a grand scale.

---

[1] For some account of drawings of this sort see Damie Stillman, 'British Architects and Italian Architectural Competition', *Journal of the Society of Architectural Historians*, 32 (1973) pp. 43–66.

[2] A history of such academies in Italy and elsewhere is given in Nikolaus Pevsner, *Academies of Art, Past and Present* (Cambridge, 1940), pp. 140–2, and Carlo Pietrangeli, *L'accademia nazionale di San Luca* (Rome, 1974).

The only possible departure from the ideal nature of these competitions was that of 1711 for a new sacristy for St Peter's, which can be seen as a distant trailer for Marchionni's building, eventually begun in 1775.[3] As dilettantes and connoisseurs, both Robert and James disqualified themselves from any of those competitions, though Robert Adam was nodded into the Accademia di San Luca in 1757, as well as those of Florence and Bologna. Amongst the drawings which the brothers produced before their respective departures, were several projects which probably fall into the *concorsi* category, in much the same way as did Chambers' mausoleum designs, made in Rome in 1751.[4] But unlike Chambers' elaborate and careful watercolours, the Adams' pen and wash drawings in the Soane Museum, were an odd assortment of which, few were in any sense finished drawings, and others, barely disguised drawing lessons. Amongst them were a series of related sketches and designs for the Westminster Parliament by James Adam, a few for rebuilding Lisbon by Robert and a large, miscellaneous and scattered group of overlapping schemes for a royal palace, probably by Robert Adam. All of them fit some of the criteria as *concorsi* schemes, except few were finished and almost all were conceived as more or less serious propositions. Buildings as it were in waiting. For this reason, they were different from Robert Mylne's *concorsi* drawings of 1758 for idealised Grande Piazze, or those four years later by James Byres for an equally hypothetical palace.[5] The Adam schemes did, however, offer a synthesis of the teaching of Clérisseau and Piranesi and the less intellectual influences of Dewez and Lallemand, and because of the almost impractical nature of such designs, they captured, all the more vividly, the theoretical spirit of mid-eighteenth-century architecture.

The *concorsi* taught lessons about composition on a grand scale as well as current or fashionable architectural theory. Their means were conventional ones – plans, elevations, sections and perspectives – but because they were paper schemes, draughtsmanship and the correct drawing style were of supreme importance. No doubt, neither Robert nor James Adam needed to be reminded of that, but, otherwise, they were probably out of sympathy with the *concorsi* emphasis on the impractical and superficial. For the Adam brothers to invest time and money in a project, the scheme had to have some hope, however, sanguine, of realisation. That was why Lisbon appealed to Robert, and the Houses of Parliament to James. On top of that, the brothers too had

---

[3] For the Concorso Clementino see, Paolo Marconi, Angela Cipriani, Enrico Valeriani, *I disegni di architettura dell'Archivio Storico dell'Accademia di San Luca*, 2 vols., (Rome, 1974), I, p. 11, pls. 242–55; and Joachim Gaus, *Carlo Marchionni* (Graz, 1967), pp. 67–103.

[4] Harris, *Sir William Chambers*, pp. 24–314.

[5] Marconi, *I disegni*, I, pp. 20–1, pls. 535–6, 605–11.

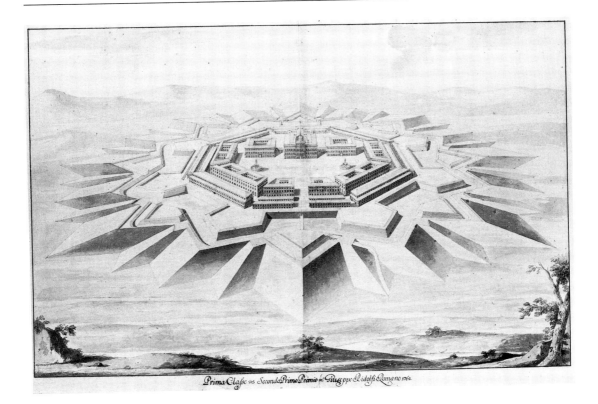

Prima Classe ≈ Seconde Primo Premio ≈ Giuseppe Ridolfi Romano 1762

Figure 33 Giuseppe Ridolfi, *Veduta prospettico, Concorso Clementino, 1762*

little truck with the impersonal character demanded of all the *concorsi* schemes. The remote, monumental air of the competition drawings after 1750, which more or less excluded figures and street-life on any scale or extent, was very different from Adam ideas of what a successful architectural perspective should convey (figure 33). The perspective of Giuseppe Ridolfi, first equal prize winner of 1762, showed the sort of impersonal geometrical style on which Adam turned his back, when making his perspectives for the Admiralty screen or The Adelphi, where vivid street-life counterpointed the buildings.[6] Such crowds were thinned to a trickle in his later picturesque inventions but they were always present. It was the human element, certainly instilled by Piranesi, that made such perspectives increasingly different to the severe and cold drawing style, cultivated by the *concorsi*, towards the end of the century.

Volume IX of the Adam drawings has pasted into it the important caption cut from some dismembered sketchbook: 'These Sketches before this were done abroad, those that follow are done since my return to England. Janr. 1758.'[7] The hand was that of Robert Adam, but it is hard to determine how many such

---

6 *Ibid.*, p. 21, fols. 587–91.
7 The inscription itself has been cut from some notebook and added to this volume, possibly from the despoiled sketchbooks which make up this section itself, as has the further note to f. 72.

41

Figure 34   Robert Adam,
Sketch for a palace

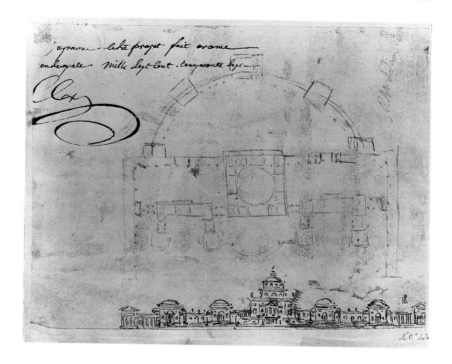

books were despoiled to produce the seventy-one surviving drawings. The draughtsmanship of many of them is a problem too. The sheets seem to represent several drawing exercises, probably associated with Dewez, and on the theme of a centralised building. But amongst them are the few drawings which have been linked with Adam's scheme for Lisbon of 1756. That they have turned up in such a compilation probably points to their original purpose as part of a largely theoretical exercise in town planning inspired by the recent earthquake in Portugal. Such a scheme may possibly have been suggested to Adam by Dewez, aware of *concorsi* schemes like the city by the sea, of 1732. Any such project was of course dependent on Clérisseau's approval as the pompous note, 'j'aprouve cette projet', on a small pen sketch of 1757 for a palace, made quite plain (figure 34).[8] Such an academic role for the Lisbon scheme probably accounted for the unusually flippant and facetious tone of Adam's letters to his family where it was discussed, and his surprise when his remarks were taken at face value. His opening letter to his sister Betty, in 1756, was that 'my

---

[8] For this see Marconi, *I disegni*, I, pp. 15–16, pls. 377–84. The first prize was gained by the Turinese architect, Bernardo Vittone. The text for the competition was probably devised by Antoine Derizet, who had won a *Prix de Rome* in 1723 and had taken part in the *concorso* of 1725. The drawing was inscribed, 'j'aprouve cette projet fait a rome an de grace Mille Sept Cent. Cinquante Sept'. (*Architectural Drawings in the Victoria and Albert Museum*, p. 33. This drawing can be related to several of the theoretical schemes in Soane Museum, AV IX.)

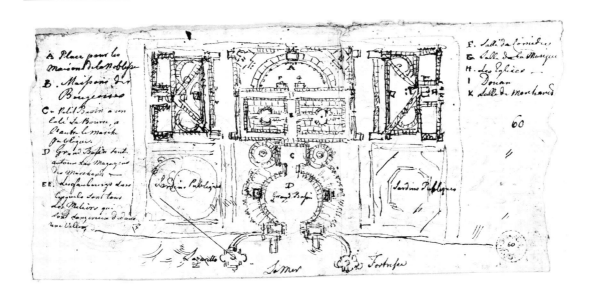

Figure 35   Robert Adam,
Proposed plan for Lisbon

resolution of going to Lisbon is drole enough, & was I a man with a high character & a white beard, I dare say I should do very well there' but later that year he made it quite clear that the Lisbon project was 'always considered a desperate one', and joked about it as such.[9] Only a prankster would have considered making the financially feckless William Adam 'treasurer general to all our works there'.

There is only one drawing in this group which appears directly related to Lisbon. It is a pen sketch which outlines a bay with the estuary of a river flowing into it, along with a fort on one of the adjoining headlands.[10] This could well be Lisbon and the Tagus copied from some contemporary map. Apart from this, there are two other sketches which can be associated with the Lisbon project – one is a town plan and the other a bird's-eye view (figure 35).[11] Both are on different sorts of paper and the more important plan has a key annotated in French. To these can be added several other drawings which have particular elements of the Lisbon design in common. Altogether, these drawings represented a series of studio exercises where a variety of themes were treated as essays in architectural composition. A tiny sketch plan for Lisbon, probably by Dewez, was the start of some such lesson which produced its own variations of different parts of the scheme. Three of the circular plans in this first part of the volume, may well be enlargements of the bourse or public auction which flank the inner basin of the harbour, noted 'C' in the plan key.[12] There were other

[9] SRO GD 18/4799, 4809.   [10] AV IX, f. 56, verso.
[11] *Ibid.*, ff. 56, 60.   [12] *Ibid.*, ff. 31, 36, 37, 39.

drawings too, some worked out to scale and on the drawing board which could be variations of the hemisphere of the aristocratic quarter, marked as 'A' in the plan.[13] Added to them, were several elevational sketches which showed how the bird's-eye view might have been developed. One of these was a small pencil drawing which gave a tantalising glimpse of the city at 'A', with a piazza and fountain in the foreground, domes and porticoed buildings behind and in the distance the flanking churches identified at 'H' (figure 36).[14]

Whether Dewez had competed in such *concorsi* in the past is not clear, though his putative master Vanvitelli had been a member of the Academy since 1732. Vanvitelli also had connections with Lisbon where he had designed a chapel in the church of San Rocco in 1743 and had collaborated earlier with his father in producing a panoramic view of the city.[15] Something of this may have rubbed off on Dewez who, since his arrival in Rome, had seen two *concorsi*, that of 1750 for a College of Arts and Sciences, and a further one for a temple-cathedral in 1754. The 1758 *concorso* for a *grande piazze con portico monumenti commemorativi* was probably known as he sat drawing with Robert Adam. The subject for the *concorsi* was always announced well in advance and certainly several months before any submission date was set.[16] For Dewez to obliquely encourage Adam's interest in such prestigious affairs seems likely enough, and the Lisbon scheme was perhaps the ideal way to do it. Topical and showy, able to be supervised by an experienced hand and coming at the right time, it suited Adam to the ground. The project had too the international slant of some of the *concorsi* which for all their abstract nature were often influenced by events in and out of Italy. For example, the Turinese architect Sacchetti's project of 1757 for the quarters around the new Royal palace at Madrid may have suggested to the academicians of San Luca a subject in the next *concorso*.[17] Seen the other way around, the Madrid design may itself have been descended from Juvarra's winning design in the 1705 *concorso* where the subject had been a royal palace.[18] In this fashion, some of the incomplete Adam schemes for a centralised building may well have been suggested by the 1754 *concorso* where the subject set was a cathedral. Rather closer to the Lisbon project were the titles for both the 1732 and 1738 *concorsi*. The subject for that of 1732 was a city

[13] *Ibid.*, ff. 58, 59.

[14] *Ibid.*, f. 45 verso. The eventual solution to the rebuilding of this quarter was two squares linked by the Riva Augusta and bound on the sides by the Riva d'Ouro and da Prato, which roughly approximate to a geometric version of Adam's scheme, see George Kubler and Martin Soria, *Art and Architecture in Spain and Portugal* (Harmondsworth, 1959), p. 115.

[15] Jorg Grams, *Disegni di Luigi Vanvitelli* (Naples, 1973), p. 27.

[16] Pietrangeli, *L'Accademia*, pp. 284–6.

[17] Kubler and Soria, *Art and Architecture*, pp. 44–5.

[18] Richard Pommer, *Eighteenth-Century Architecture in Piedmont* (New York, 1967), pp. 47, 48, 70.

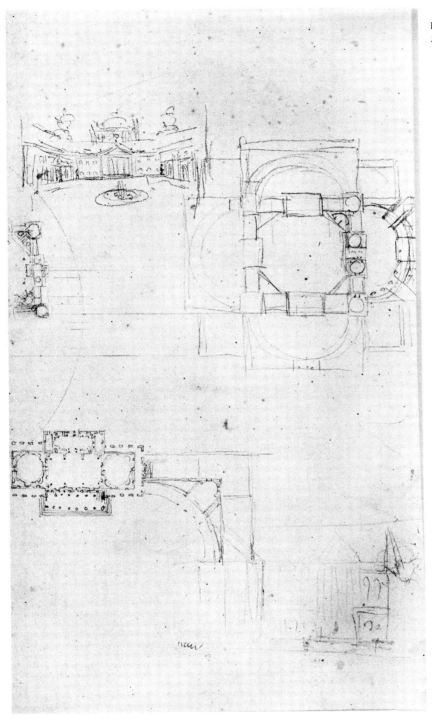

Figure 36 Robert Adam,
Sketch perspective of Lisbon

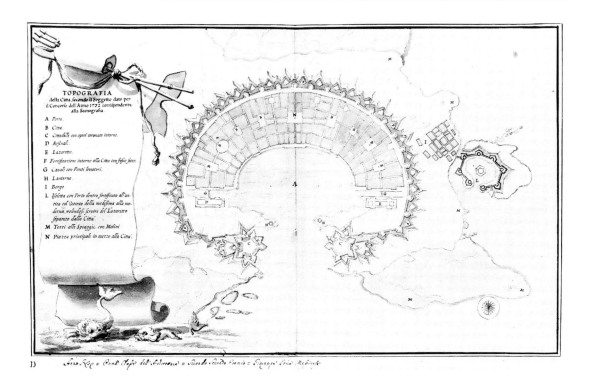

Figure 37 Giuseppe Doria, *Topografia della Città, Concorso Clementino, 1732*

surrounded by the sea, and this had produced in its second prizewinner Giuseppe Doria a design grounded in the recent planning improvements of his native Messina (figure 37).[19] Such a coupling of the real with the conjectural was repeated in the 1738 competition for a large piazza in a city on a river, where the winning designs echoed contemporary town plans both Italian and European. The more imaginative response to these *concorsi* can probably be found in Piranesi's stupendous harbour or his *magnifico Collegio* from the *Opera Varie*, of 1750, putting in the shade the mediocre schemes successful in the *concorso* for that year for a College of Arts and Sciences. Piranesi of course floated above such routine performances of the Academy and arrogantly claimed that his scheme was derived from the '*Palestre de Greci, e Terme de'Romani*'.[20] He and Clérisseau no doubt encouraged in Adam such a lofty and condescending attitude to the notion of public competition.

The Adam scheme for Lisbon shared with the *concorsi* designs of the fifties a strong liking for exact symmetry and a visual hierarchy. There were distant echoes of this, in the later, and more sophisticated quarter plans he produced for Glasgow and Edinburgh, and more intimately at The Adelphi. His only seaside

---

[19] Helmut Hager, *Architectural Fantasy and Reality: Drawing from the Accademia Nazionale di San Luca in Rome* (Pennsylvania, 1982), p. 110.

[20] G. B. Piranesi, *Opera Varie di architettura* (Rome, *c.* 1750), 'Pianta di ampio magnifico Collegio'.

port that cast a backward glance to Lisbon and the *concorsi* was the small scheme for the development of Mistley in Essex as a bathing establishment in 1774. An even fainter echo was the diminutive form of the *basin circulaire* that appeared beside the Firth of Forth in Adam's 1774 perspective for Barnbougle (figure 38).[21] But, like all pieces of eighteenth-century planning, the roots for these and the Lisbon scheme lay deep in the renaissance, as for that matter did most of the *concorsi* designs. Vittone's winning scheme of 1732 showed very clearly in its central piazza with its radiating rings, its debt to renaissance planning as well as pointing forwards to the pattern that Piranesi adopted for his *magnifico Collegio* design.[22] The same pattern can be seen in the Adam sketch for Lisbon where the fort and lazzaretto which guard the entrance to the Grand Basin were repeated inside on a smaller scale. Such a regard for paper geometry was characteristic, too, of all three successful schemes for the seaside city *concorso* of 1732. In this, they were fully in step with contemporary architectural developments, of which Vanvitelli's work at Ancona on the harbour, forts and lazzaretto was perhaps outstanding. It seems reasonably certain that Adam studied even if he did not draw all of them in 1755, and Dewez would have been aware of the distinction

Figure 38   Robert Adam, *Perspective of the east elevation of Barnbougle Castle*

---

[21] See p. 152.

[22] For Vittone and his 1732 scheme see Paolo Portoghesi, *Bernardo Vittone* (Rome, 1966), pp. 89–95, and Hager, *Architectural Fantasy*, pp. 109–10.

Figure 39   Robert Adam,
Plan for a Royal palace

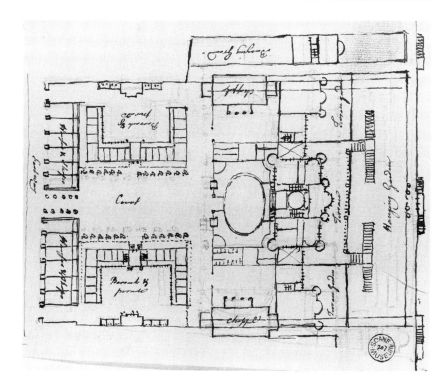

of the lazzaretto, if only through the Vasi engraving of 1738.[23] Where Adam and Dewez seemed to have departed from such prototypes was in the planning of the Lisbon inner city. They tried to avoid the rigid, grid pattern which placed churches and piazze at strategic points, found in so many of the *concorsi* schemes. Outstanding in this but in few other respects was Carlo Sala's chequerboard plan for the 1732 competition.[24] Adam adopted a different, less balanced, and more complex pattern, using large and small piazze and little or no grid structure. His plan, too, showed no particular limit to the city unlike the confining walls and bastion of all the Italian designs. Instead, Adam proposed public gardens on either side of the grand Basin and intended the other parts of the city to be developed at some future date. Such a limited, piecemeal approach was of course true of the later rebuilding of Lisbon itself.

Lacking in the Lisbon sketch was any royal palace, though the proposed noble quarter would suggest an appropriate spot. The *concorso* scheme for the city by a river lacked a similar provision but as all the *concorsi* were under papal patronage this omission was hardly surprising. More typical of them was the *Palazzo del*

---

[23] See Marilena Pasquali, *Il lazzaretto di Luigi Vanvitelli* (Ancona, 1980), pp. 58–85.
[24] See Marconi, *I disegni*, 1, pp. 15–16, pls. 385–97.

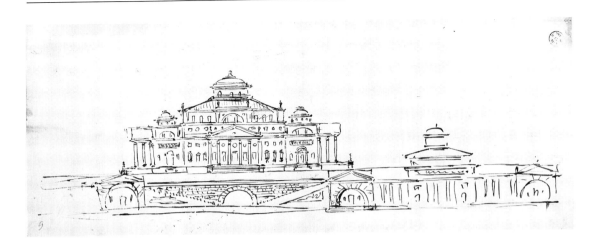

Governatore della citta from Carlo Sala's competition plan.[25] Such a particular distinction can probably be taken further, for Adam's Lisbon was a strongly mercantile, almost presbyterian city with emphasis on the *douane* and *salle de marchands*, the *Magazins des marchands*, the bourse, public market and a quarter for the bourgeoisie, with little attention paid to the church and its appendages. Adam had no cathedral or bishop's palace. However, he may have toyed with the idea of a royal palace, for amongst the Soane drawings in volume XXI, there was a small sketch plan, carefully annotated in ink to show a barracks and parade ground, chapels, burial ground, terrace and hanging gardens (figure 39).[26] The last would suggest Lisbon rather than riverside London as a possible setting for this palace complex. Near the edge of the sheet, at the opposite end from the gardens, the plan was zoned for houses and shops which together formed an archway and avenue to the palace. This was a development which continued perhaps where the Lisbon sketch plan had left off. And it may have extended to a rough pen elevation for a palace building whose ramped terraces, possibly descending to the Tagus, perhaps associates it with the riverside palace plan (figure 40).[27] Certainly, Adam's composition here of a tiered structure crowned by a Pantheon-style dome, rather like a grandiose Palladian scheme of the sixteenth century, was typical of his compositional methods at this time. It

Figure 40 Robert Adam, *Sketch elevation for a riverside palace*

25 *Ibid.*, pl. 385.
26 Soane Museum, AV XXI, f. 207. Volume XXI is a collection of designs for various buildings and in the W. L. Spiers 'Catalogue of the Drawings and Designs of Robert and James Adam', of 1909, they are given as 'Sketch Plans' on p. 31. Those that have been identified are for British commissions and are dated between 1759 and 1778. Folios 202 and 203 may possibly be refugees from volume X.
27 Soane Museum, AV X, f. 17. It is also possible that this design belongs with ff. 2–19 and could be related to the Robert Adam Parliament scheme (ff. 12, 15); folios 1, 20 are clearly for some sort of palace, and dated 1756, see Fleming, *Robert Adam*, pl. 48.

corresponded well with the sort of buildings suggested in both his Lisbon bird's-eye view and his slight pencil sketch. The contrast between this tentative Lisbon palace and his Piranesian concoctions found in the same volume, could hardly be more complete, though the basic geometry of the balanced pyramid was much the same.[28] What was absent from the palace scheme, was any sop to reality beyond its supposed setting. Adam's palace elevation, more so than the plan, read like some lesson in a phase of architectural history, and a rather breathless statement about what he had mastered and was set to master.

Both Robert and James Adam were unusually close-mouthed about contemporary Italian or Roman architecture and its practitioners, apart perhaps from Vanvitelli. They were equally guarded in their praise. They did, however, readily appreciate the scale and grandeur of eighteenth-century architecture and the obvious role the *concorsi* had in fostering a taste for public magnificence as well as the importance of papal patronage. It was, after all, Clement XI who had endowed the competitions in 1702, and they lasted virtually as long as Rome remained a papal state. Though the city declined throughout most of the eighteenth century, the flurry of building works sparked off by the Holy Year of 1750 could not have escaped at least Robert Adam's attention while that of 1775 saw the start of Marchionni's vast new sacristy at St Peters.[29] In the course of *The Works*, Adam rather reluctantly recognised this aspect of patronage when he wrote that 'The bigoted zeal and superstitious pomp of the Roman Catholic religion have produced a like profusion and magnificence in the public works of modern Italy; and to that cause, however incompatible it may seem to be with general science and liberal ideas, Italy owes its vast progress and present splendour in the arts of elegance.'[30] He can hardly have helped comparing such an achievement with the dead hand of Presbyterianism or even Anglicanism, and the lack of stimulus these churches had given the arts in Britain in the past. Such limitations of state patronage had produced a public deprived, Adam maintained 'of that emulation which is excited by public works'.[31] If indeed, 'Public Buildings are the most splendid monuments of a great and opulent people', as he wrote in *The Works*, then the role of the *concorsi* and such competitions was an essential part of an equation where, at the end of the day, theory could well turn into practice.

There can be little doubt that all the *concorsi* schemes were theoretical ones, made to display unknown and unexploited talents. Occasionally, they were taken further for one reason or another, and this appeared to have been the case

---

[28] Soane Museum, x, f. 18
[29] *Rome: La città degli Anni Santi, 1300–1875* (Rome, 1985), pp. 316–33.
[30] *The Works*, part IV, p. unnumbered.
[31] *Ibid.*

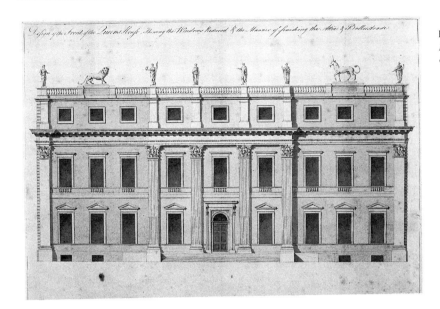

Figure 41   Robert Adam,
*Design for the Front of the
Queen's House*

with Adam's royal palace. Perhaps it was a scheme close to his heart. It may,
too, have satisfied his increasing thirst for public recognition as well as his more
altruistic concern to raise the standards of architecture and taste in Britain, all as
it were, in one fell swoop. He had, after all, publicly trailed his coat for such
patronage. In the preface to *The Ruins* he had made much of George III's
enthusiasm for architecture and how it would encourage 'every lover of his
Profession to hope he shall find in George III not only a powerful Patron, but
a skilful Judge'. He continued, with rather less conviction, that he anticipated
such a reign to become the equal to that of Pericles, Augustus, or the Medici.
The commission from the King to remodel the garden front of the then Queen's
House (Buckingham Palace) in 1762, had encouraged more than just the
obligatory flattery of *The Ruins*' preface, and misled Adam into replacing the
small, and old-fashioned building with something much grander and closer to
the scale of his Lisbon scheme.[32] Apart from some work in the interior of the
palace, Adam's practical proposals were limited to the reduction of the windows
and the recasting of the attic and balustrade. Little of that was ever carried out
and his drawing differed little from Chambers' rival scheme for refacing the east
front of the same date (figure 41).[33] At the same time, he roughed out his ideas

32 The Queen's House was altered between 1762 and 1769, see Harris, *Sir William Chambers*, p. 83,
    and H. M. Colvin (ed.) *History of the King's Works* 6 vols., (London, 1976), V, p. 134.
33 The surviving drawing is at Hovingham Hall, Yorkshire. It is captioned 'Design of the Front of
    the Queen House shewing the Windows as Reduced & the Manner of finishing the Attic &
    Ballustrade'. For Chambers' proposal, see Harris, *Sir William Chambers*, pl. 116.

Figure 42 Robert Adam,
*Sketch plan for the Queen's
House*

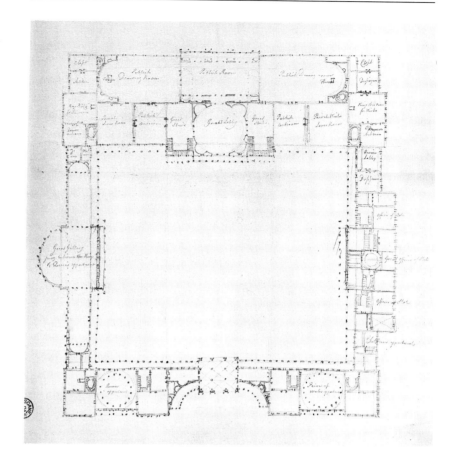

of how the palace could be made to justify its title. His surviving sketch plan
showed him simply taking over the existing 'U'-shaped building of the main
block and quadrant pavilions and doubling it around a courtyard, much as had
happened in the seventeenth-century expansion of the Louvre (figure 42).[34]
The notes to Adam's plan showed an attempt to construct a similar social and
architectural balance, as he had done at Lisbon, equating the Queen's apartments with those of the new Prince of Wales (born 1762) and forming a 'Great
Gallery joining between the Kings & Queens apartments'. In keeping the King
in his existing apartments, in the old building, Adam spoilt the functional and
ideal symmetry of his scheme as well as obviously bowing to his royal client's
well-known conservatism and parsimony. The elevation that has survived for
the proposed palace was a straightforward Palladian design with a giant portico
and dome above, marking the entrance to what Adam termed, the Great Lobby
and the King's Apartments. It was not greatly different in style to the entrance

[34] Soane Museum, AV LIV, series VII, f. 135.

of Adam's Register House, of 1774. The approach to the palace was through a triumphal arch carrying the identifying inscription 'Georginus Terzo Rex', above the central arch (figure 43).[35] There could hardly be a greater contrast between this clear and basic piece of planning, without much movement or any subtle manipulation of space, and his fluid, Piranesian daydream palace schemes of about five years earlier.

Robert Adam produced another and larger version of this palace scheme in pen and ink, possibly around the same time. It was for a much grander palace, without any historic core, and unrecognisable except for the repetition of the King's and Queen's apartments in approximately the same spot as the smaller Queen's House plan.[36] Apart from that, the drawing might well have been a distinct rival for the projected palace at Richmond on which, gallingly for Adam, William Chambers was at work in 1762 (figure 44).[37] Nothing further seems to have come of Adam's sketch proposal for a building divided into four

Figure 43 Robert Adam, *Triumphal arch for the Queen's House*

35 *Ibid.*, ff. 136, 137. There is also an incomplete pencil plan and elevation, ff. 138, 139.
36 Soane Museum, AV IV, f. 138. The King's And Queen's apartments are in the same spot as in AV LIV, series VII, f. 135.
37 See Harris, *Sir William Chambers*, pp. 77–80; and Colvin, *King's Works*, V, p. 225.

Figure 44   Robert Adam,
*Plan for a Royal palace at
Richmond*

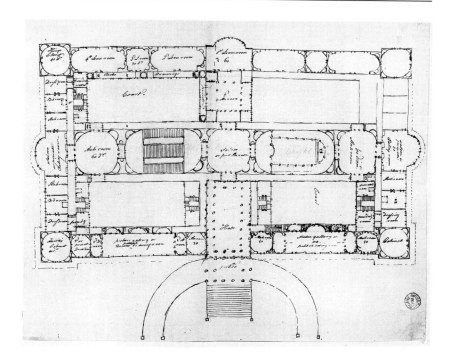

courts in the style of Vanvitelli's Caserta, or Ferdinando Fuga's Neapolitan
Albergo dei Poveri which Adam would have seen when in Naples, in 1756. The
entrance arrangement of portico and hall was much in line with his other
scheme, though the interior of the entrance hall was expanded to dimensions
similar to that of Kedleston. He did, however, produce one variation upon it,
in which the square courts were made circular in the style of Inigo Jones'
Whitehall Palace, and the entrance planned in some detail and to scale.[38]
Nothing came of such possible bids for greater royal patronage, just as nothing
in the end came of Chambers' Richmond Palace. What made these designs
more than intrinsically important were their sensible, perhaps humdrum
qualities, for Adam seems to have responded rapidly to the sharp realities of
architectural practice in London. There was not, in that commonsense
approach, a great deal to choose between the Chambers' double-courted plan
for Richmond and Adam's sketch for a palace with four courts (figure 45).
Perhaps surprisingly, for Chambers was a thoroughly professional designer who
had had ten years to digest his Roman experience and adjust to the limitations
of British patronage. At this stage, Adam seems to have turned his back, for the
time being, on the dramatic and immensely varied sorts of plan that Piranesi had
offered, as well as Clérisseau's picturesque view of architecture. Instead, there

[38] Soane Museum, AV IV, f. 156, and AV X, ff. 6, 8.

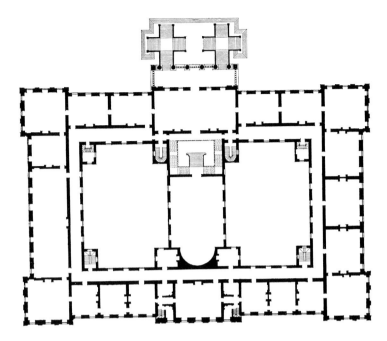

Figure 45   William Chambers, *Plan for Richmond Palace Two*

was in all these schemes, loosely derived from the Lisbon enterprise, the heavy groundswell of Dewez's orthodox classicism expressed clearly and composed concisely.

Throughout 1762, James Adam had struggled in Rome with the task of designing a new Houses of Parliament for London. This was his 'great design', his *concorso*, about which he suggested without apparent irony that his brother 'Bob cannot better employ a leisure hour than in sketches of such a work which if ever set about seriously in England might turn out very useful in adjusting a great design'.[39] The role of architectural adjuster must have been a new one for Adam, though he and Dewez had probably acted out similar parts in the tentative stages of the Lisbon scheme. That such a design might prove useful was to remain part of the Adam calculations for quite some time. It was recognised, generally, that there was a pressing need to extend, if not rebuild, the existing palace at Westminster, and this had been apparent since William Kent's work there in the 1730s.[40] In finding for James Adam a survey plan of the existing Parliament and a list of the various offices associated with it, Adam had come across the Kent drawings. He had been appointed in 1761, as architect of the King's Works and so had access to such drawings, for Westminster was

[39] SRO GD 18/4932.
[40] For Kent's scheme, see Michael Wilson, *William Kent* (London, 1984), pp. 168–71.

administratively a royal palace. Presumably, at this time, he made the rough copies that remain in the Soane Museum which he may have used in turn for his own design for the Edinburgh Register House.[41] They may also have filled the hypothetical 'leizure hour', for there are certainly about sixteen pencil drawings of plans and elevations for a Parliament scheme, belonging to around 1770, when such a rebuilding became, once again a practical possibility.[42] That these drawings appeared together in a separate volume from those of James Adam's similar designs − volume VII − makes Robert Adam's authorship reasonably certain. They bear looking at closely, for they show Adam continuing and expanding the ideas aired in his royal palace schemes of the 1760s. Several of the compositional schemes were taken further in Adam's later public works in Edinburgh, Cambridge and in London, at Lincoln's Inn.

There can be little question that these drawings were for a Parliament scheme, and that they follow on from the unfinished Roman design made by James Adam, some six years earlier. The final, but undated, last word on all of these drawings both by Robert and James appeared in a large, rough, pencil and wash perspective endorsed on the back, 'Parliament Ho: Last Design' (figure 46).[43] This enormous building seen from the Thames, was recognisable compositionally from all the earlier schemes of the brothers. If James Adam's plan of 1760 was followed, the main block was divided into three, with a central and domed Painted Hall, balanced on either side by the Judiciary and the Lords and Commons.[44] The river elevation was dominated by an elongated cupola, over the entrance to the Painted Hall, with the great bulk of the dome just behind. This pattern was repeated on flanking blocks with a similar silhouette glimpsed in the Speaker's House, vaguely washed in, at one end of the drawing. In this way, it offered four distinct elevations, each with a changing scale and strong scenographic character. Some of the related but, unfinished drawings, in volume VII, reveal something of the scale of the design and they point, again, to an ancestry in James Adam's putative *concorso* scheme (figure 47). The entrance portico to the Painted Hall was over ninety feet long and this element of vast

---

[41] Soane Museum, AV IV, f. 179. The Kent plan was copied both by Adam and Soane for their respective schemes. (Soane Museum, drawer 36, set 2.) For Soane's work on the Houses of Parliament see Colvin, *King's Works*, VI, pp. 499, 520. It is possible that Adam may have been influenced in his Register House design of 1774 by the Kent drawings, see A. A. Tait, 'The Register House: Robert Adam's Building', *Scottish History Review* (1974), pp. 115–23.

[42] Soane Museum, AV X, ff. 2–18; between 1768 and 1770, a new Court of Requests and a new building on St Margaret Street were built (Colvin, *Kings Works*, V, p. 249). It is possible that the sanguine Adam, viewed this as the start of a wholesale rebuilding of Westminster.

[43] Soane Museum, AV I, f. 28. There is a similar but earlier plan, f. 29, which does not altogether match this elevation.

[44] *Ibid.*, AV VII, ff. 1–4.

Figure 46   Robert Adam,
'Parliament Ho: Last Design'

scale was a common denominator with all the earlier Parliament designs.[45] It also shared a strongly formal, public quality (though perhaps not the size) with William Kent's schemes for Westminster of the 1740s. Like them, it successfully used a repeating rhythm of almost standard units. The effect was, nonetheless, an Adam rather than Kent exercise in movement and variety – concepts well aired in the prefaces to *The Works* – which emphasised in neoclassical fashion the different functions of the great office block. Such clarity was apparent, too, in the simple planning of the interior where a corridor ran from the Justice Hall, through the Court of Requests and Painted Hall to the Parliamentary portico and revealed a breathtaking vista of the English constitutional system (figure 48). It was, in every way, the ideal *concorso* project and perhaps sufficiently conjectural to have allowed the composition to float free from the restraints of the practical, in all but a token sense.

Certainly this was probably Clérisseau's reading of the project, if not entirely that of James Adam, whose slow and self-conscious attempt to match the style and draughtsmanship expected of such a competition entry had delayed – if not paralysed – the completion of his drawings. Though in 1762 he had begun to recast his sketch designs, only the entrance elevation was fully finished in the end, and the rest remained more or less as fragments on his departure from Rome the following year.[46] In setting aside this year for revision and drawing,

[45] *Ibid.*, f. 3.

[46] In October, Adam wrote that 'I have not an Elevation yet finished & my great Section is also but little advanc'd so you see I have really no more than my plan compleat. Now to hasten it I have put another two hands on it' (SRO GD 18/4949).

Figure 47   James Adam, *Plan for the Houses of Parliament, Westminster*

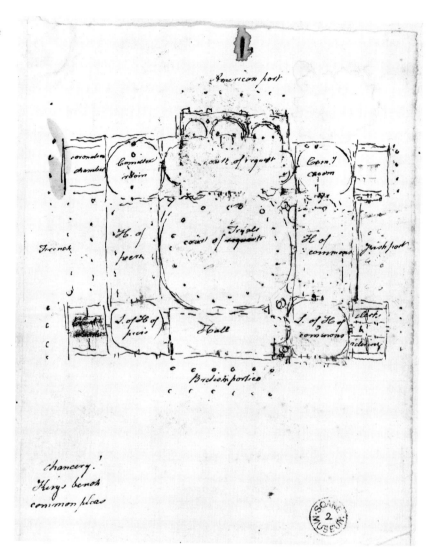

James Adam and his assistant, probably George Richardson, had not left themselves a great deal of time. The Scottish architect and prizewinner, Robert Mylne reckoned that his *concorso* designs 'cost me 7 months hard study', a pace that James Adam was unlikely to sustain even with Clérisseau's encouragement. From the outset, both he and Clérisseau probably realised the useful discipline of the *concorso* and the advantage to be had in shadowing the *palazzo per un principe*, the subject of the 1762 competition. Possibly James Adam's Roman associate and fellow collector of architectural fragments, his amanuensis James Byres, who won third prize, may have nudged Adam in this direction. To have competed outright would have spoilt the Adam disguise of the

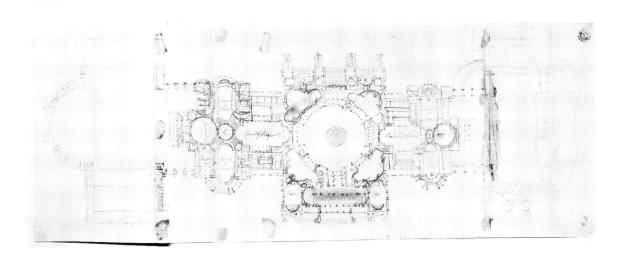

dilettante. It was under such gentlemanly cover that he, the Abbé Grant and probably George Richardson, all visited the Accademia di San Luca especially to see Mylne's 'Academy prise' of 1758, and possibly his bizarre thanks-offering – an altarpiece dedicated to 'Humilitas' and 'La Devotione Accademia S. Luca' (figure 49).[47]

Figure 48   Robert Adam, plan of 'Parliament Ho: Last Design'

The Houses of Parliament were James Adam's putative *concorso* subject, adapted to his needs by Clérisseau who set the standards and style of its draughtsmanship. The project was not strictly a theoretical one and did have a purpose, for it was developed against the background of renewed interest in rebuilding Westminster. Such a possibility remained tenaciously part of the Adam scheme of things for some time and public patronage of this sort was still pursued in the 1778 preface to part v of *The Works*.[48] An illustration of the Parliament scheme was probably meant to have been included there and to have complemented James Adam's engraving of the Britannic Order which was to have embellished the building (figure 50).[49] The brothers had great faith in James Adam's Parliament design and they seem to have adopted it as a collective essay in the grand style. It was certainly the most impressive of James Adam's Italian drawings which were remarkably thin on the ground, that is outside the Parliament drawings contained in volume VII. It seems unlikely that there were ever a great deal more, for the arrangement of this album was an old one, probably from around 1816 and before the last Adam sale. It appears to

[47] Stillman, 'British Architects' p. 49. The Mylne drawing is in the Cooper-Hewitt Museum of Design, New York, 1930–88–4049; for the competition drawings see, Marconi, *I disegni*, I, pls. 535–6.

[48] *The Works*, I, part v, pl. 2.

[49] See pp. 114–15.

Figure 49   Robert Mylne,
Design for an altarpiece, 'Ex
Devotione Accademia di S.
Luca'

Figure 50   James Adam,
*Design of the Entablature and
Britannic Order*

have been quite deliberately and authoritatively put together as a record of his
independent work. It included some of his juvenilia of 1752, as well as one of
his rudimentary, academic life drawings, of possibly 1761 which was certainly
inferior to his brother's (figure 51).[50] There were no drawings in the volume

50 *Seated youth with rope* is in Soane Museum, AV VII, f. 186; there is a further, and much better,
    drawing of the same model possibly by Pecheux in the Blair Adam Collection. The rest of the
    drawings in volume VII are more or less in chronological order. His villa plan and elevation of
    1752, f. 16, were followed by a 1756 design (f. 17) and there was a ceiling design for Bowood
    signed 'J.A. Arch.', which must be of about 1764. Folios 223–9 in this volume include the designs
    for the octagon in Lower Grosvenor Street.

Figure 51 James Adam,
Seated youth with rope

later than those for Lansdowne House where he had collaborated with his brother for the first time on his return from Rome. The Parliament projects that the volume contained included two drawings for 1760 and a revised plan and elevation, probably of the following year, all of which served as a source for the grand design of 1762.[51] To these must be added the possible copy elevation, perhaps redrawn for the unmade *Works* print, of James Adam's final scheme which has now been separated from them and added to volume XXVIII (figure

---

[51] Soane Museum, AV VII, ff. 1–2, for the 1760 scheme: ff. 3–4 for the revision of that of probably 1761.

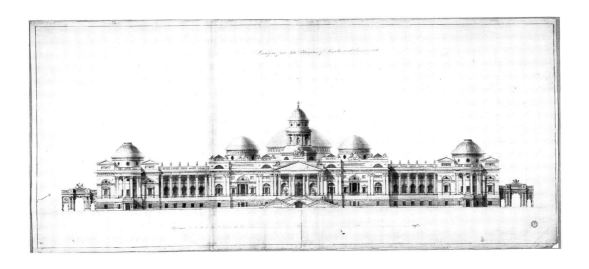

Figure 52   After James
Adam, elevation of a 'Design
for the Houses of Lords and
Commons'

52). Along with these architectural drawings were a series of washes for the relief panels and sculpture that were to ornament the building.[52] None was obviously in James Adam's hand and they were more likely to be the work of his assistant Antonio Zucchi, or of the two Giuseppes, Sacco and Raffaello, who had accompanied James Adam on some of his drawing trips. Most of these bold and handsome drawings were made at the end of 1762, or even the start of the following year, when James Adam was still at work on the scheme.

James Adam's first thoughts on paper showed a central and circular 'Court of Tryals', with the Lords and Commons on either side, each with their own courtyard (figure 47). The building had four porticoes – British, French, American and Irish – of which the central pair, American and British, gave access to the vast Court of Trials. The succeeding scheme was much the same, except the central court had shrunk to become the smallest of the three, with the larger pair each embellished with an arcaded walk for illustrious persons round a circular fountain (figure 53). The four porticoes reappeared but with the American and British ones made larger and more prominent, setting up an important cross axis to the river. The plan was exactly, almost ruthlessly symmetrical and in this way quite different from the Adam Lisbon scheme. The arrival of the Office of Works memorandum, from Robert Adam in London, put an end to these ideal schemes. James wrote to his sister in 1762 that he hoped his brother 'has got the plan I have so long wished for. Now that my own plan is made out my curiosity to see the old is greater than ever.'[53] Presumably his own plan referred to the second scheme for which there also existed an

[52] *Ibid.*, AV VII, ff. 47–59.   [53] SRO GD 18/4929.

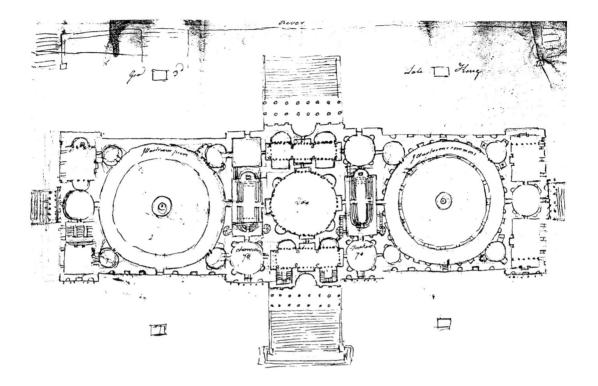

Figure 53 James Adam, *Plan for the Houses of Parliament, Westminster*

incomplete and lavishly decorated elevation in a self-consciously antique style (figure 54). This was pruned and simplified, probably by Clérisseau, in the *concorso* style to become the large elevation that has remained in the Soane Museum (figure 52). It was possibly during this revision that James met with his 'vast difficulties', and complained that 'I have not an Elevation yet finish'd & my Section is also but little advanc'd so you see I have really no more than my plan compleat. Now to hasten it I have put another two hands on it.'[54] The other hands presumably finished the surviving elevation, or a copy of it, and on that hung James Adam's reputation as an architect in the grand style. The elaborate section-elevation, demanded by the *concorso* rules, was probably never completed and the remaining details and variations for the entrance portico were possibly as far as the section had advanced. The plan 'still improving', in 1763 has apparently disappeared.

James Adam in his unfinished historical essay of November, 1762, wrote that 'decoration is a part of architecture', and went on to define decoration as 'sculpture, statues, and bas-reliefs, together with foliage, trophies, frets, inter-lacings'.[55] This set out an interpretation that was diametrically opposite that of

[54] *Ibid.*   [55] Fleming, *Robert Adam*, p. 317.

64

the Venetian rigorists and possibly closer to Piranesi's revised idea on the role of ornament. The Parliament schemes and his engraving for the Carlton House screen of 1767, were all faithful to such ideas and this was borne out by most of the surviving drawings by Zucchi and indeed by James Adam's capital for the Britannic Order (figure 55).[56] His immediate Roman inspiration was from the Villa Albani, whose architect Carlo Marchionni had incorporated antique fragments into the facades and was still working in the same picturesque vein on the so-called Greek temples there. The Villa Passionei, where James Adam bought antiquities, showed a similar eclectic attitude to the past with fragments incorporated into the structure, possibly under Clérisseau's direction.[57] Such decoration, he felt gave dignity to building and as he later wrote in *The Works*,

Figure 54 James Adam, *Incomplete elevation for the Houses of Parliament, Westminster*

[56] See pp. 67–8.
[57] For the Villa and its association with Clérisseau, see McCormick, *Clérisseau*, pp. 52, 99–100; and for James Adam's antiquities, p. 78–81.

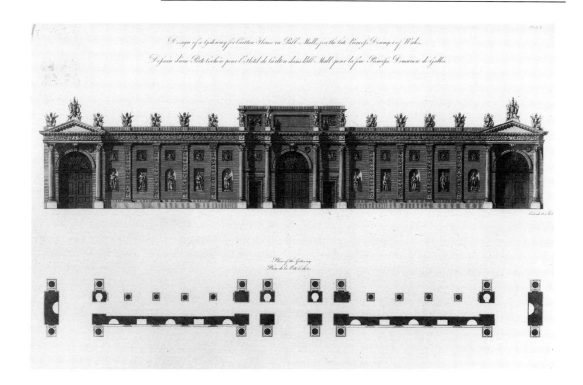

Figure 55 James Adam,
*Design of a Gateway for Carlton
House in Pall Mall*

'was the necessary accompaniments of the great styles of architecture'. This fusion between theory and practice proved irresistible to James Adam and it was certainly more appealing than the exacting business of plain architecture or the tedium of architectural drawing. Like many architects before him, he confused decoration with design. His drawings in this particular volume for sculpture and painted grisaille panels went hand in hand with his writing of the theoretical essay. They overlapped to the extent that the quadriga that crowned the entrance pediment of the Parliament was referred to in the text of the essay, and Zucchi's relief panels mentioned in the same way.[58] These panels however, illustrated modern rather than classical history and, logically enough, the highlights of English history, running from King John and the Magna Carta to the current exploits in the colonial wars against France in Canada, India and the West Indies (figure 56). It was only through the clarity and symbolism of such elaborate decorative programmes that Adam felt recognition would be possible for his building two thousand years hence, though here he was arguing against the lesson of history.

His Parliament drawings were largely finished by March, 1763. They were shown around his Roman circle where they were seen and praised by Piranesi,

[58] Fleming, *Robert Adam*, p. 318.

probably not for the first time.[59] This was to be expected, but rather more surprising was the seriousness with which the project was treated. It was accepted as James Adam's private *concorso* submission and criticised accordingly, though probably sympathetically. Piranesi was reported as seeing in it 'the true Spirit of Antiquity' which was captured in 'the contrivance of every Ornament for it'.[60] This was approval as much for Adam's eclecticism as his own attitude to ornament, aired by him in his *Parere su l'architettura*, of 1765. It was possibly a relief to Piranesi to find a like mind, for the militantly classical drawings produced for the *concorso* of 1762 can hardly have pleased him. Those of the prizewinner, Francesco Lavegna, showed elevations without significant ornament and drawn with severity, and much the same spirit was apparent in those of Giuseppe Ridolfi, the other prizewinner (figure 33).[61] Such neoclassical austerity was even more pronounced in the succeeding *concorso* of 1766. Against them Adam's drawing must have seemed conservative and comforting. Perhaps for those reasons, Piranesi referred obliquely to the grand scheme in the *Parere* as possessing in the Britannic Order the mastery of the sort of ornament and variety about which he had written.[62] Why he should have seen a parallel between the idiosyncratic Etruscan style that illustrated the *Parere* and the staid classicism of Pantheon domes and Corinthian order of James Adam's surviving elevation, was a mystery only explained by Piranesi's combative nature. Whatever the shortcomings of James Adam's scheme, it was still closer to Piranesi's current thinking than that of his critics. James Adam was an ally who had found favour with Didascolo in the *Parere*. Perhaps nearer were Robert Adam's fantasy palaces of 1756 (figure 57), but neither brother grasped the

Figure 56   Antonio Zucchi, 'Martinique Bombarded, April, 1762'

59   Damie Stillman, *English Neo-Classical Architecture* 2 vols., (London, 1988), I, p. 56.

60   *Ibid.*

61   Marconi, *I designi*, I, figs. 587–91.

62   Piranesi, *Parere su l'architettura* (Rome, 1765), p. 13; and John Wilton-Ely, *The Mind and Art of G. B. Piranesi* (London, 1978), pp. 77–9.

Figure 57 Robert Adam,
Elevation for a palace

inventive and allegorical classicism of Piranesi's designs for Santa Maria del
Priorato, though they had copy drawings of the facade and altar (figure 58).
Piranesi's opinion in 1769 that, 'by prudently combining the Grecian, the
Tuscan, and the Egyptian together', the resourceful architect 'ought to open
himself a road to the finding out of new ornaments and new manners', was only
imperfectly heard by James Adam.[63] If the years between 1760 and 1765 marked
a radical turnabout in Piranesi's architectural thinking, away from the pursuit of
simplicity and the tenets of rigorism and towards the cult of ornamentation, then
he was at an intellectual crossroads in his comments on Adam's Parliament in
1763.

It is unlikely that Piranesi had much involvement with any of James Adam's
three Parliament schemes. He was too impatient for the painstaking coaching
that James Adam needed, though he was quite possibly disingenuous when he
claimed in March, 1763, that he had seen the plan for the first time. Much of
the overall direction rested with Clérisseau and practical help in draughtsmanship came from Zucchi and Richardson. It was to Clérisseau rather than Piranesi
that James Adam probably referred in his remark about seeing his new plan
'from the lights I have been able to pick up here'.[64] Certainly, the classical
backbone of the Parliament scheme came from Clérisseau though the strong
sense of movement in the Adam facade and central organisation cannot have
appealed to him as much as it did to Piranesi. Clérisseau's flat drawing for the
facade of the Chateau Borély, of 1767 showed, in contrast, the restrained way
in which he used ornament and hinted at movement (figure 59). But in his way
of drawing, James Adam was closer to Clérisseau than his brother whose palace
drawings of 1756 and 1757 were vigorous and lively and revealed greater

[63] Piranesi, *An apologetical essay in defence of the Egyptian and Tuscan Architecture* in *Diverse maniere
d'addornare i Camini* (Rome, 1769), p. 33.
[64] SRO GD 18/4929.

Figure 58   Anonymous,
*Unfinished drawing of the facade
of Santa Maria del Priorato,
Rome*

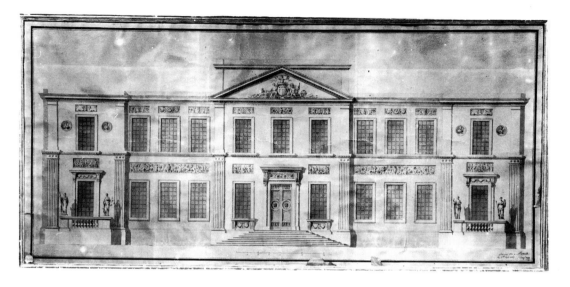

Figure 59 C. L. Clérisseau,
*Design for the facade of the
Chateau Borély, Marseille*

susceptibility to Piranesi's influence (figure 57). The triumphal arch, Roman Baths, Palladio and the renaissance cloister, all strung together in Robert Adam's 1756 palace displayed a stylistic flexibility worthy of Piranesi. Such an imaginative sweep and its lack in James was the fundamental difference in the Roman work of the two brothers. This contrast was repeated in their different drawing styles where, despite the same teaching, James Adam's careful, thin hand, with its use of watered ink and small regular hatching suggested uncertainty and lack of confidence. If this was his mental state, then that rather than time or resources was why he failed to complete his *concorso* Parliament and later hesitated to engrave it for *The Works*.

So much then for the Adam brothers' training in the style of the *concorso*. The absorption of such lessons was gradual but complete and the large office perspectives for the later proposals of the Haymarket Theatre or Lincoln's Inn carried their impressive hallmark. Such palace and Parliament schemes were the final statement in their visual education that had started from first principles in the Roman drawing academies. Each brother had been encouraged by Clérisseau to look beyond pure draughtsmanship and see their drawings as revealing the variety and mood of the design that existed in their minds. These were not technical or intellectual abilities that either of the brothers picked up quickly or easily. Perhaps, one of the more important motives in forming their joint collection of drawings, paintings and antiquities was to be able to use some of it as an *aide-mémoire*, not only for the stalwarts in the office but for themselves. Though much was sold and dispersed, as they intended, a substantial core remained to stimulate the brothers' imaginations and provide a constantly evolving response to such abstract Adam concerns as variety and mood.

3

The Adam office

IN 1789, MARGARET ADAM wrote from London to her niece expressing her concern for the well-being of the Adam drawing collection. 'The depravity of the servants in this place', she wrote, '& things that are left in this house are not like what other people leave behind them because the Books & drawings are like the Stock in trade & are at the same time very perishable'.[1] Much the same fear often surfaced in Adam's own letters to his clients or their agent where he warned against his drawings 'being copied or going into bad hands'. In their varying ways both sister and brother pin-pointed the drawings collection as the key to the Adam styles. Therein lay what Robert Adam termed 'the whole Soul, Body and Guts'.

Such a serious approach to collecting drawings was an essential development of the Adams' Italian experience and was quite different from the usual architectural practice of keeping drawings as a record or *liber veritatis* of some sort. It was also more than just a grand tour phenomenon, for the brothers continued to acquire drawings – their own, those of assistants like Manocchi and, as the sale catalogues suggest, contemporaries such as Sandby and Gainsborough. In this they were hardly exceptional and no match for dedicated artist-collectors such as Reynolds or Lawrence. They outdid, however, most architects like Hawksmoor or Chambers who did collect drawings reasonably consistently.[2] Unlike such collections too, that of the Adams was an open-ended one, for Robert Adam maintained that his Roman topographic drawings were to be 'of use for drawing after and for giving hints to the imaginations of we modern devils'.[3] While this was certainly true, it was hardly the whole story. A collection so assiduously formed was intended for higher and better things than just copying. The drawings acquired by Robert and James Adam in Italy, for

---

[1] SRO GD 18/4961/15.
[2] D. J. Watkin (ed.), *Sale Catalogues of Libraries of Eminent Persons: Architects* (London, 1972), pp. 81–98; and Harris, *Sir William Chambers*, p. 184.
[3] Fleming, *Robert Adam*, p. 152.

whatever motives, were in many ways an attempt at a history of drawing and draughtsmanship from the renaissance via the seventeenth century of Cortona to the contemporary manner of Clérisseau and Lallemand. Such a collection showed as much the techniques of architectural composition and individual style as the broader artistic developments of the day. This breadth of understanding made James Adam in 1764 the acceptable arbiter on the quality of the Albani drawing collection for both Lord Bute and George III.[4] For the novice entering the Adam office for the first time, the collection played a different, more tantalising tune. It taught composition and notation, and revealed drawing standards past and present which gave the astute apprentice a clear insight into the sources of the Adam styles. By such means, he could – had he any ability – analyse and refashion the Adam style as did Richardson, Bonomi, Robertson and Morison. This was both a strength and danger to the brothers.

Both Robert and James Adam returned to London with collections in which drawings were an important though possibly expendable element. Rather like the pictures and antiquities, the drawings had been bought haphazardly and often for a seemingly contradictory range of motives. Possibly they were a commercial venture, acquired with more than half an eye on the auction room and in expectation that some of their investment might be quickly recovered, as the sales of 1765 and 1773 made all too plain. Such a speculative element did not exclude the collection's more pedagogic purpose which was to initiate the green draughtsman into the achievements of architectural drawing, past and present. It made clear what could be achieved and showed the means. In forming such a collection, the brothers revealed their curiosity about the history of architectural draughtsmanship in the broadest sense, as well as their dedication to the principle of learning by analysis and example. The various sale catalogues of the collection showed large, basic holdings of the work of their Roman contemporaries, Clérisseau, Lallemand, Piranesi, Pecheux, and smaller groups by view-makers such as Panini and the familiar Marco Ricci, from earlier in the century. The common bond was, loosely, the architectural or topographic drawing, stretched to include the manuscripts they owned by Vasari, Montano and Fontana.[5] They all worked hard for their living and Carlo Fontana's compendium of seventeenth-century theatre designs had a direct bearing on Adam's schemes for the Drury Lane theatre or the Haymarket opera house (figure 60).

The collection was documented beyond the limited information of the sale catalogues by a miscellaneous Soane volume, called, appropriately enough, a

---

[4] John Fleming, 'Cardinal Albani's Drawings at Windsor', *Connoisseur* 142 (1958) pp. 164–9.
[5] Bolton, *Architecture*, II, p. 330; they were acquired by Sir John Soane at the 1818 Adam sale.

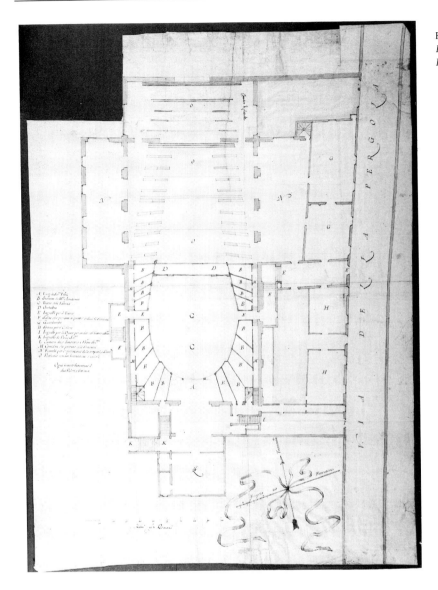

Figure 60   Carlo Fontana,
Plan of the Teatro della Pergola,
Florence

scrapbook. It varied substantially in quality and the range was considerable. At best, it included the stylish drawings of the Trevi Fountain from Robert Adam's Roman survey, the two schemes of William Kent, and a rather battered design for a tomb in the Venetian church of the Madonna dell' Orto (figure 61).[6] Of lesser quality was a copy after Claude and an incomplete pen drawing by Lucio

6   Soane Museum, AV LVI, ff. 55–7, see p. 138, AV LVI, ff. 42, the last was inscribed 'Disegno del sepolcro nella Chiesa della Madonna SS.a. Dell Horto', dated 1701 and signed 'Cavdagno Inv.'

73

Meus of Titian's *Presentation of the Virgin*, which was meant to be coloured up according to a given key.[7] The heterogeneous nature of the volume emphasised the wide – if not indiscriminate – range of the brothers' collecting zeal and the refinement of their taste as well as a sharpening of their eyes. It also reinforced their cover as the scholar-connoisseur, masking, should it show, their too professional interest in architecture. However, in the end, both Robert and James Adam viewed all their Italian acquisitions with a sharp and calculating eye, ready to keep any part of the collection that flattered their taste or acumen but equally disposed to sell should the right opportunity present itself.[8] The whole range of pictures, drawings and antiquities was there to support, in every sense, the architectural practice rather than the other way around. Robert wrote to his sister Peggy in November, 1755, that 'I believe I will be master of a very pretty little collection well chosen & cheap, In so much that I am fully convinced on selling one half of my pictures at London, I shall have t'other for nothing at least.'[9] Much the same opportunistic pleasure surfaced in a letter by James Adam from Venice. He wrote in 1760 that 'As to the pictures what ever way they come to your hand, it is to be understood that all risks are on my account & half of all profits are on yours, for I should have little pleasure in my purchases if I thought you were to be no gainer by them. There may be several of these pictures I should wish to keep, in which case I will point them out to you.'[10]

Neither brother waited long to put his expertise to the test. Any delay there was between moving to Lower Grosvenor Street and the first auction in 1765, was to do with bringing the collections together and letting some dust settle on their illicit arrival. In Robert Adam's case, his pictures and antiquities had been brought in, without duty, on the understanding that they were all part of his architectural studies and this subterfuge had to be 'a dead Secret' and kept 'snug that there was pictures'.[11] The best paintings were then cleaned and framed in carved and gilt wood and objectively reckoned by Adam to be 'a little collection which no Nobleman in the land would be ashamed of'. The sale was to be a three-day one in February at Prestage's in Savile Row whose catalogue made much of both the Adam provenance and the nature of the collection. That the paintings had been assembled by them 'during a stay of eight years in Italy, France and Holland', distinguished it as a connoisseur's rather than a dealer's questionable hoard.[12] If nothing more, it proved the relative success of their

---

[7] Soane Museum, AV LVI, ff. 159, 40.

[8] John Fleming, 'Messrs Robert & James Adam Art Dealers (1)' *Connoisseur* 144 (1959) pp. 168–71.

[9] SRO GD 18/4792.

[10] *Ibid.*, GD 18/4868.

[11] *Ibid.*, GD 18/4852.

[12] *A Catalogue of the genuine, large and valuable Collection of Italian, French and Dutch Pictures, belonging to Robert and James Adam, Esqs* (London, 1765), pp. 1–4.

Figure 61 L. Cavdagno, 'Diesgno del Sepolcro fatto nella Chiesa della Madonna SS.a. Dell Horto'

dilettante disguise. The auctioneer, probably under instruction, singled out certain lots which with the exception of Zuccarelli and Fyte all belonged to the sixteenth and seventeenth centuries, and were overwhelmingly Italian as might be anticipated. If this sale catalogue was read in conjunction with the following one, at Christie's in 1773, a distinct pattern emerged of the brothers' conventional and less than marketable taste. But remarkably enough the prominence which both Prestage and Christie gave to the Adam name and provenance in their catalogues, suggested that they must also have shared the brothers' over-rosy expectations.

In investment terms, none of the Adam sales during the brothers' lifetimes – that is those of 1765, 1773 and 1785 – can have been a true success and provided any significant return on their investment. Indeed, they can only have brought them unwelcome publicity, at the wrong time. The first sale was without doubt their best with seemingly three-quarters of the lots sold, but in the succeeding one of 1773 roughly 52 out of 114 lots were bought in and reappeared in 1785.[13] In this last auction, held at Christie's, 73 paintings were nominally sold for £329, though several were certainly bought in by the auctioneer. Such a reading of the figures would give an average price of about four to five pounds a painting. The outstanding exception was Ludovico or Annibale Carracci's *The Entombment of Christ, attended by the Three Marys*, which although offered in the earlier sales was sold to Nixon for £29–8–0 in 1785.[14] More typical of the Adam luck was the Celesti, *Sophoristia drinking the poison*, unsold in either 1765 or 1773, which was ultimately got rid of as a Cleopatra, for twelve shillings.[15] All of this was a far cry from James Adam's valuation in 1762 of his holding of 500 paintings at £4 each, which he reckoned, with typical Adam optimism, would increase in value five times to £20 in the next ten years.[16] Clearly this did not happen, nor was Robert Adam any more fortunate especially when he anticipated a return of a hundred per cent on the pictures imported to London in 1758. Indeed, for it to have happened in the way that the brothers predicted, would have been flying in the face of all odds, for the return of £5 was perfectly in line with contemporary prices fetched by wallpaper or furniture Old Masters.[17] The 1773 Adam sale of both pictures and antiquities raised £3,429, of which £1,494 had to be

---

[13] For the Christie's sale of 1773, see Bolton, *Architecture*, II, pp. 324–5. The 1785 sale was not noted by Bolton, but the priced catalogue for 9 June 1785 made clear the number of paintings reappearing from 1773. *A Catalogue of a capital Collection of Pictures and High-finished drawings, the Property of Mess. Adam*, (London, 1785), pp. 1–7.

[14] It appeared in the 1773 sale as Ludovico, and in that of 1785 as Annibale, and described there as 'the subject finely expressed' (lot 69). It was perhaps one of the three Carraccis that Robert Adam bought in Bologna in 1757, Fleming, *Robert Adam*, p. 233.

[15] The Celesti was lot 18 in the 1785 sale.

[16] Fleming, *Robert Adam*, pp. 296 and 377.

[17] See Louise Lippincott, *Selling Art in Georgian London* (New Haven, 1983), p. 64.

Plate 1 Robert Adam,
Garden Monument,
watercolour after the Tomba
del Somaro, Rome

Plate 2 Agostino Brunias,
*Elevation for the Breakfast
Room, Kedleston*

Plate 3 Adam Office,
'Sketch of a Coloured
Ceiling', King's Box, Drury
Lane Theatre, London

Plate 4   Robert Adam, *Castle on a rock approached by figures*, watercolour

Plate 5 Robert Adam, *Primitive seat for Mrs Kennedy at Dalquharran*, watercolour

Plate 6   Robert Adam, *Sketch for landscaping the park at Kedleston*, watercolour

Plate 7   Robert Adam, *Sketch design for Bambougle Castle*, watercolour

Plate 8 Robert Adam, *Sketch proposal for a castellated gate and lodge for Drummond Castle*, watercolour

Plate 9 Robert Adam after John Clerk, *View of Crossraguel Abbey*, watercolour

Plate 10   Robert Adam, elevation 'in the style of an Italian Casino or Villa', watercolour

spent on bought-in lots, against a valuation of £6,649 given the year before.[18] At no time did either of the brothers candidly admit the questionable value of their collection as little better than the average London picture dealer's. Perhaps the only note of reality was a posthumous one, when William Adam wrote to his nephew about the 1818 auction of the rump of his brothers' collections: 'Italian pictures sell for nothing now, but the people present said the things sold well & better than was expected'.[19] But certainly not well enough to rest the expectant shades of his two brothers.

The general role of the Adam collection, pictures, drawings, antiquities, was to personify the Adam taste until its sublimation in the Adam style. The character of the collection was to be matched in every sense by their evolving architecture. Its range and eclectic nature was an effective advertisement of the Adam attitude to a broad classicism, which was interpreted as a way of thinking rather than as a set of rules and precedents. The public display of the collection was intended to be the first gust of the approaching Adam storm that was to sweep over Lower Grosvenor Street as it would Britain. For this reason, the successful fitting up of their London house was of the utmost importance, for the pictures, sold or unsold, served as an advertisement to inherent good taste. In the Grosvenor Street parlour Adam had what he termed his 'Amigonis', two landscapes by Teniers, *St Francis* by Guido Reni and a painting of 'figures riding through the Colosseum'.[20] They were reckoned by him to be his 'tip-tops', presumably the most eye-catching and marketable, as well as being appropriate to the room. Perhaps surprisingly, they were not sold by 1765 when the two Amigonis appeared in the auction catalogue as *Angels washing St. Veronica's Handkerchief*, and its companion *Charity*. The Teniers were possibly the catalogue's *Mary Magdalen in Landscape* and *St Peter in Landscape*, and the Guido was a *Head of St Francis*.[21] The 'figures riding through the Colosseum' would suggest Panini but there was nothing fitting such a description in either of the 1765 or 1773 sales. Adam's dining room had his Domenichino, Carlo Maratta, *St. Catherine* by Guido and some other choice pieces.[22] The Domenichino was the very large *Allegory of Time*, probably bought in Bologna in 1757, the Guido Reni a small *St. Catherine*, acquired in Rome, and the Carlo Maratta can probably be identified with the only one in the 1765 auction, a *Holy Family* on copper.[23] His

[18] Blair Adam Muniments, 4/21 and 232.
[19] *Ibid.*, 4/2.
[20] Fleming, *Robert Adam*, p. 251.
[21] Prestage sale, first day lots 59, 60, second day lots 64, 65: third day lot 70. The catalogue described the Guido Reni as 'very fine'.
[22] Fleming, *Robert Adam*, p. 251.
[23] For the 1773 sale see Bolton, *Architecture*, II, pp. 324–8. In 1785, the Domenichino (lot 68) sold for 10 guineas and the Guido Reni (lot 66) for 5 guineas.

absolute confidence that he could readily dispose of these parlour pictures was misplaced. Few were sold in 1765 and more failed to reach the reserve Adam had placed on them. Only one of the parlour Amigonis was sold outright. The situation in the dining room was not really much better as the Domenichino, Reni and Maratta all turn up again in 1773, as did the Domenichino and Reni in 1785. The sad history of the Guido *St. Catherine* was typical of the misfortunes of the whole collection. Adam had acquired it in Rome and rashly claimed that 'not having cost me £20', it was worth at least 200 guineas.[24] It was a hostage to fortune, for in the end, it was disposed of for five guineas. For whatever reason – subject, quality or price – Adam was clearly out of step with the contemporary London market. Possibly the strong religious or moral tone of much of the collection and that also a great many of them were the work of the late Baroque, did not make their sale in England any easier.

Apart from the pictures, the other sizeable investment by the brothers was in the antique. Once again, the acquisitions made in this field were for a wide variety of motives quite apart from their respect for the antique itself. Though they bought the run-of-the-mill casts, as any architect would do, they were much more interested in original pieces, genuine or old copies, which gave them a sort of copyright as well as an intrinsic value in the market place. The two Adam sales that included the antique were those of 1773 and 1818. That of 1785 had been devoted to paintings with the addition of a few Etruscan-style vases designed by Robert Adam. The auction of 1773 was centred around pieces that James had bought and were largely sculpture. The later sale of 1818 consisted of Robert Adam's casts and a few examples of architectural sculpture. What was on offer were works that James Adam had bought in Rome, disappointingly from the traditional Roman collections rather than from the new finds explored by his antiquarian associates James Byres and Gavin Hamilton. His notebook, presumably of 1762, listed the 'Good Antiquitys yet to be procur'd at Rome' and gave a brief account of the major collections – Mattei, Albani, Rondanini, Giustiniani, Barberini, Spada, Lancellotti, Massimi, Furietti and della Valle.[25] Within the palaces that housed them, he singled out pieces that appealed to him and which he might be interested in buying, should the price be right. His cautious nature always sought the obvious, and in these collections he was attracted by the Apollo Verospi and the Barberini Faun, now in the Munich Glyptothek (figure 62). A bas-relief and bust of Pompey from the

---

[24] Fleming, 'Messrs Robert & James Adam', pp. 169, 171. Fleming doubts that such a picture 'could hardly have been sold for so little as £20 in 1756'.

[25] SRO GD 18/4945. The Mattei was one of the collections that James Adam noted as where 'Good Antiquitys yet to be procur'd at Rome'. He had in mind encouraging George III to buy that collection and wrote home asking that 'His M may be spoke to & would begin a marble collection by so great a stroke', (*Ibid.*).

XCIV.

STATVA D'VN BACCO ritrouato sotto L'Pontificato d'Vrbano VIII. trà le rouine della Mole Adriana nello scauar il terreno per far le fondamenta delle nuoue fortificazione del Castello S. Angelo.
Nel Palazzo Barberino.

In Roma nella stamp.ᵃ di Dom.ᶜᵒ de Rossi alla Pace, con Priuil.ᵉ

R.V. Auden Aerd delin. et Sculp.

Figure 62   Barberini Faun, after Maffei's *Raccolta di Statue antiche e moderne* (1704)

79

Spada, a vestal from the Palazzo Lancellotti and even some antique chairs in the choir (possibly the two marble thrones) of San Giovanni Laterano, all caught his acquisitive eye.[26] Where he smelled a bargain, he could be surprisingly quick off the mark. In July, 1761 he visited the Villa Passionei, probably at Clérisseau's suggestion, where the Cardinal had recently died and his antiquities were 'begun to be pulled all down, and the whole was to be sold'.[27] He returned a month later, in August, and offered 205 crowns for an urn supposedly from the Villa Adriana and some other fragments, but was unsuccessful for nothing more was heard of them. The two candelabra from the Passionei collection that did appear in the 1773 sale were both classed by the auctioneer as 'modern'.[28]

Some of his other successes can be identified from the 1773 sale catalogue. He did, in fact, buy some sort of Barberini Faun as well as a Jupiter rather than Apollo from the Verospi, and even some of the mosaics he had admired in Cardinal Furietti's collection.[29] In such transactions the limiting factor was not availability, but price. James Adam reckoned that if he had spent £6,000 on antiquities, it would have increased in nine years to £30,000, though such a speculative valuation should be taken with a pinch of salt. To justify such optimism, he maintained that a small statue that he was buying on commission for the Duke of Northumberland for around £150 (including freightage to London) would have cost between £250 and £300 on the London market.[30] On the eve of the antiquities sale of 1773, he still 'had great expectations from these and the statues & other Antiquities, as both these classes are allowed to be the best of their kind exhibited in England'.[31] Such optimism was not justified and the Adam sculpture was sold with about the same success as their pictures. Of the 104 lots of sculpture offered in 1773, nearly a quarter reappeared in the 1818 sale.[32] Amongst those were two urns and a carved sarcophagus front, possibly from James Adam's collection, that were bought by Soane for £37. This must surely have represented a loss to the Adam brothers on any terms (figure 63).[33]

Sadly the brothers' taste as either collectors or connoisseurs rarely rose beyond the conventional. Nor was there a great deal to choose between them, and both collections had similar themes and strengths. Perhaps that was to be expected

---

[26] *Ibid.* Both brothers shared an acquisitive enthusiasm for the Venetian Grimani collection and tried in 1757, 1758 and 1760 to buy the colossal statue of Marcus Agrippa. (Fleming, 'Messrs Robert & James Adam', p. 171.)

[27] *Library of The Fine Arts*, II, p. 117. Clérisseau may have designed a 'Folly' there for the Cardinal before 1751. (McCormick, *Charles-Louis Clérisseau*, pp. 16–17.)

[28] Bolton, *Architecture*, II, p. 327.

[29] *Ibid.*, p. 328.

[30] SRO GD 18/4951.

[31] Blair Adam Muniments, 1454/4/184.   [32] See Bolton, *Architecture*, II, p. 333.

[33] In the 1818 sale, Soane bought the antiquities in lots 94, 96, 97 and the sarcophagus, lot 115.

Figure 63   Five cinerary urns and sarcophagus panel: the panel centre and extreme right urns probably from James Adam's collection

for they had similar budgets and a common need for source material which restricted further their originality and enterprise. But even when they were buying for others, such as Lord Shelburne or the Duke of Northumberland, there was little radical departure except perhaps in price. They seem to have been reluctant to capitalise on the expertise of Hamilton or Byres. Although James Adam certainly bought drawings largely of antique subjects from both of them, the extent of their influence was hidden by the customary Adam pall of secrecy (figure 64).[34] Neither brother showed a particular interest in Byres' Etruscan finds nor demonstrated any significant enthusiasm for Hamilton's pioneering study of Italian painting before Raphael, which produced the 1773 *Schola Italica Picturae*.[35] Such originality was treated with the same tepid caution and lack of comprehension as the more radical ideas of Piranesi. The brothers'

[34] Byres arrived in Rome in May, 1758 where he had a career as a guide and dealer. He was associated with James Adam in both respects and there are several of his drawings after the antique collected together in Soane Museum, AV XXVI, ff. 166, 167, 170, 174, 176. (F. 167 was inscribed 'Mr Buiers at Rome'.) A design for a contemporary chimney piece was noted 'From Mr Buiers at Rome', (f. 183).

[35] Gavin Hamilton returned to Rome in 1756 and both Robert and James Adam were on dining terms with him. In the Adam sale of 1818, amongst the books were listed 'Sundry prints from Hamilton's Etruscan Antiquities', though these are more likely to have been prints of William Hamilton's *Collection of Etruscan, Greek and Roman Antiquities*, (Bolton, *Architecture*, II, p. 331).

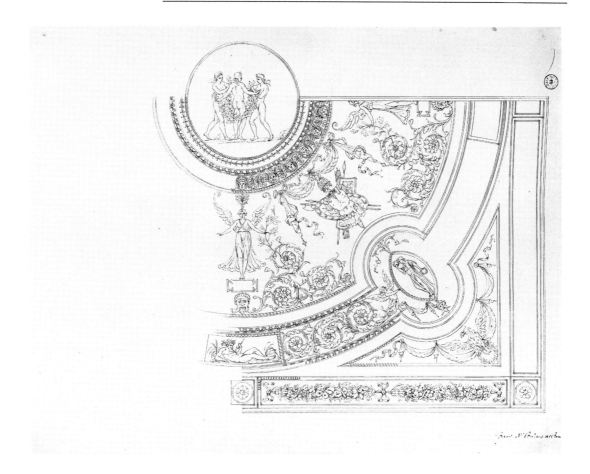

Figure 64 James Byres,
*Ceiling drawing after the
Antique*

collecting was too ruthlessly practical and unadventurous to be successful, and too hurried to be lucrative. Nothing showed this better than their attitude to the ornamental drawings in the Guise collection whose acquisition James Adam recommended principally as 'useful weapons in our hands & very dangerous in the hands of others'.[36] All of this fell short of the exaggerated ambition of 1756 when Adam wrote half-seriously that 'with money I'd transport to England the Pantheon & Columns of Trajan & Antonie. Let that therefore be the Chief aim'.

Robert Adam adopted much the same commercial attitude to his and his brother's antiquities as he had done to their paintings. The result was just about the same, despite their considerable promotional efforts. A small pen sketch captioned 'Manner of placing the Ancient Marbles under the Room in my area', showed the first steps necessary to make a successful sale (figure 65). The area Robert Adam referred to was the rear courtyard of his Lower Grosvenor Street

[36] SRO GD 18/4927.

82

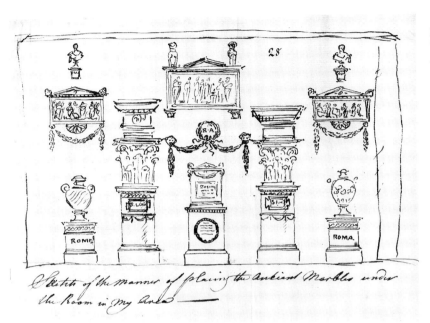

Figure 65   Robert Adam,
'Manner of placing the
Ancient Marbles'

house and the drawing showed a symmetrical mixture of reliefs, urns, capitals, lion masks (acquired in 1755) and busts set on one of the walls.[37] Such pieces were matched by similar ones from James Adam's collection. A surviving drawing on coloured paper for a sarcophagus was noted as 'Ex Museo J.A.', and probably referred to one of his acquisitions displayed there (figure 66). Like the rest, it was informally for sale, less so when the sarcophagus appeared as lot 20 in the 1773 auction.[38] A rather more sympathetic and ambitious setting for some of the larger antiquities, may have been offered by a small casino that was proposed for the end wall of the courtyard. There remain a handful of drawings for it, mostly office copies after James Adam, which show an octagon of twenty-seven feet with a coffered, Pantheon dome, much in the style of Adam's garden buildings at Kedleston in 1761.[39] The source for them all was a small, rapid,

---

[37] Fleming, *Robert Adam*, p. 251.

[38] The sarcophagus was identified in the sale catalogue as 'An urn or Sarcophagus with marine figures in bas-relief, ⁹⁄₁₀ × ½' which sold for £12–1–0, (Bolton, *Architecture*, II, p. 328). A drawing of this is in AV XXVI, f. 55.

[39] See Bolton, *Architecture*, I, p. 127; Soane Museum, AV VII, ff. 213–14, 224–8. That the drawings appear in this volume strongly suggests that the design is by James Adam as does the draughtsmanship of several of the drawings. The panels in the style of the Vatican stanze are in Soane Museum, AV VII, f. 211 and match the manner of the principal pilasters of the octagon (see f. 223). The renaissance style chimney piece is shown in f. 224. According to the *Survey of London*, no. 76 Grosvenor Street was 'a house which they appear to have altered but which is now long demolished' (*Survey of London, The Grosvenor Estate in Mayfair* 40 (London, 1980), p. 56 and plate 15.

Figure 66   James Adam,
*Drawing of a panel from an
Antique sarcophagus*

pencil sketch, probably by Robert rather than James Adam (figure 67). It was a traditional form and the descendant of a similar octagon proposed for Blair Adam back in the early 1750s.[40] Much more adventurous was the style of the interior which was to have had a startling and massive chimney piece in the manner of the Florentine renaissance. This precocious revival style was repeated in the grotesque work of the pilasters that flanked the four interior niches, themselves designed to hold the larger pieces of antique sculpture in the collection (figure 68). The source for such decorative work was as much the Vatican stanze as the Villa Madama, both of which the brothers knew well, or possibly Pisa Cathedral of which James Adam was particularly fond. Amongst these casino drawings were three long panels of grotesque work that were to have set the renaissance style of the interior in some detail (figure 69). The most likely date for this garden casino was 1764 when James Adam was back in London, active in the office and with his collection unpacked.

The arrangement of the Adam collection of pictures and antiquities in Grosvenor Street was remarkably Italian. It followed the principle of the enfilade albeit in miniature. The dining room led to the garden casino with a parallel visual progress from painting to sculpture. Something of this can be read into the surviving first floor plan of the house (figure 70). The dining room on the ground floor was hung with Adam's most showy pictures and this opened into the basement (or area) where the three walls were decorated with small pieces of antique sculpture and reliefs, much in the manner of an Italian cortile. This route was closed in visual terms by the rear wall of the casino with its sculpture-filled niches, redolent more of the Palazzo Vecchio than dingy Lower Grosvenor Street. Such a splendid and stimulating showroom was not only the brothers' and sisters' home, but also a home for some boarding draughtsmen before the removal to The Adelphi, in 1772. But, it was never forgotten by those who worked there that the office dominated their careers and even the

[40] A. A. Tait, *Robert Adam at Home* (Edinburgh, 1978) pl. 27.

Figure 67 Robert Adam, *Sketch proposal for the casino at Lower Grosvenor Street* Figure 68 James Adam, 'Sketch of one of the Niches with Pilasters'

lives of all who lived there. And, in such an office, drawing ruled. The transient draughtsmen kept alive the link between Italy and Italian drawing as did, in a more intellectual fashion, the spirit of the paintings and sculpture that surrounded the Adam assistants or 'devils'. More particularly, Grosvenor Street was a melting pot where the continual ebb and flow of such assistants kept architectural drawing and the Adam ideal of drawing in constant play. It served too as a training ground, unusual in that the office pyramid changed regularly at top and bottom with the accomplished Italian draughtsmen and the raw, Scottish 'callants' as equal grist to the Adam mill.

Robert Adam's immediate task on his return to London had been to set up his collection and establish an office where the talents of the architect-connoisseur were equally visible. Such a balance, but not the pattern, changed with the return of James Adam in the autumn of 1763, when both the collection and office establishment were simultaneously reinforced. But for Adam and

Figure 69　Adam Office,
Grotesque panels

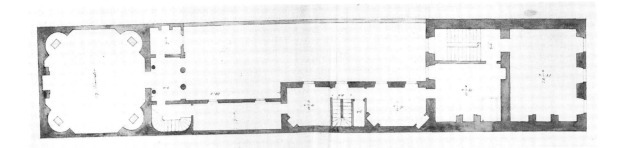

his fledgling office the years 1758 and 1759 had been critical ones. Dewez defected at the end of this time leaving Brunias as the only cosmopolitan element in the drawing room. The situation that prevailed was candidly discussed in a letter of November 1758 to James Adam, and in particular the failings of one of the former mainstays of John Adam's Edinburgh office, Jack Strahan, who 'has been now for 3 month so ill with toothach & beald cheek that he has not done a stroke of work'.[41] Adam then revealingly added, that 'even when he was well I did not find in him the least fire or ambition to become equal to his Neighbours as he never touched a pen but in the Drawing room where he was quite awkward & insufferably slow'.[42] If this was the same Strahan that Adam had dreamed of having with him in Rome in 1755, then he had declined as Adam's standards rose. He now demanded from his draughts-men speed, zeal and competition. He had been perhaps spoilt by his Roman days where he claimed that 'students of the best Italian architects want to leave their Masters in order to study in my house'.[43] Later on and in London, it could be said unkindly that the reverse was true.

James Adam's departure for Italy in early 1760 deprived Adam of Strahan's successor George Richardson.[44] This meant that for the four years between Dewez's and Richardson's departures and the return of James in October, 1763, Adam was short-handed and his office dangerously small. So much so, that George Richardson worked as a draughtsman, measurer and estimator, all rolled into one, though such versatility always seems to have been a characteristic of the office even when things improved. As a makeshift, Robert Adam seems to have followed his proposal of 1756 whereby '4, 5 or 6 Callants sett to work to drawing in John's house, as though they but copy useless things, it will be better than nothing, as I will draw them off by shipping to the Capital, as they will be both cheaper honester & more tractable than your English sons of Bitches'.[45] It is doubtful if this scheme went according to Adam's plan for one

Figure 70   Adam Office, 'Plan of the House in Grosvenor Street with the Additions'

[41] SRO GD 18/4853.   [42] *Ibid.*   [43] *Ibid.*, GD 18/4805.   [44] *Ibid.*, GD 18/4853.
[45] *Ibid.*, GD 18/4804.

of his 'Callants', had probably been Jack Strahan. A further more fanciful suggestion was to fill this gap by the 'laudable employment of procreation' and so give Adam 'a great many good Lads to draw for me in England & surely architects Bastards are the best of all for that purpose, as they will have the Genius of Kind'.[46] Such a similar hit or miss system seems to have kept the office afloat and Bonomi recalled in 1767 that there were 'amongst 10 or 12 clerks in the office under the direction of Robert Morison'.[47] But for all this, it was clear to both Robert and James Adam at the outset that a principal draughtsman was essential for the new office. It was critical as well that he had some knowledge of Italy and understood the style of draughtsmanship that the brothers so admired. In 1762, Betty Adam precisely described a regime at Lower Grosvenor Street where 'Brunias salary is about 60L, he boards for something under 40L. He seems to keep very much the same feast days with the Church of England for Bob very seldom wishes him at any other time. There is no such thing as getting a tolerable Draughtsman at under 40L salary.'[48] This was borne out by the wage paid to John Yenn of about £50 a year in William Chambers' office to do much the same. Such a salary scale was probably the key to understanding the composition of the office from the surviving but rather cryptic office accounts with their London bankers at Drummond's, Charing Cross.

The picture that emerged of the Adam office from the Bank was an incomplete and condensed one which was complicated by the brothers' speculative, building enterprises and confused by the later accounts of William Adam and Co.[49] The account was clearest for the early period, that is until the offices' removal to The Adelphi. If the figures given by Betty Adam of £40 and £60 for an experienced draughtsman are accepted, then the ledgers showed several names with a fair measure of responsibility for the offices' smooth operation. William Hamilton, Robert Nasmith, Robert Morison, Joseph Bonomi and George Richardson all belonged to this category, less so such émigré figures as Giuseppe Sacco and J. P. Laurent, who were in the office in the late sixties and early seventies. The accounts show that Hamilton was paid between 1765 and 1774, a yearly sum that ranged from £215 in 1765, to £100 in 1774, which suggested that he acted as a sort of clerk of works as well as principal draughtsman. This was true, too, of payments made to Nasmith in the 1760s.[50] Only George Richardson was given the firmer sum of £60 and

[46] *Ibid.*, GD 18/4802.

[47] Peter Meadows, *Joseph Bonomi* (London, 1988) p. 2.

[48] SRO GD 18/4950.

[49] For the complex finances of such enterprises see, Alistair Rowan, 'William Adam and Company', *Journal of the Royal Society of Arts*, 122 (1974), pp. 665–70.

[50] Drummond's Bank, 1765 ledger, f. 325, verso. The 1773 ledger showed two payments to William Hamilton, junior but this is likely to be his son the artist William Hamilton; for them see Edward

appeared to have had no further duties beyond his drawing and directing role. It may well have been that such a limitation was too restrictive and encouraged him to leave the office and set up on his own, sometime after 1770.[51] Of the foreign contingent in the office, Sacco was recruited by James Adam in Verona in 1760 and appeared in Lower Grosvenor Street by the autumn of 1765. He was paid a little over £21 in December (presumably for a half year) and irregularly thereafter, the roughly statutory £40.[52] He was gone from the accounts by 1767 and possibly replaced by Laurent who lasted two years, at about the same salary.[53] In 1768, Bonomi took his place and was paid £44 in 1768 and £54 in 1771, and presumably remained as the principal draughtsman after George Richardson left. He stayed with the office when it moved to The Adelphi and though he was associated with Adam until 1781, there were only irregular payments to him for a further two years.[54]

There were, of course, many more shadowy names who lived and died with surprising rapidity in the Adam ledgers. It can reasonably be assumed that French or Italian names were more likely to be draughtsmen than clerks or engravers, and that Louis Calas in 1765, Jean Legrix, Joseph Celeneux and Joseph Delivet in the following years, all belonged to that category.[55] Two further names appear in the accounts for this period, though neither was exclusively associated with the Adam office and both were more than just draughtsmen. Antonio Zucchi and Giuseppe Manocchi were retained by Adam as decorative artists, though in rather different capacities.[56] Zucchi appeared regularly in the office accounts from 1768 to 1771, then irregularly, with lump payments ranging from a hundred to three hundred pounds. Manocchi was paid considerably less, £127 for the 1765/6 period.[57] Each of them however, had a specific influence on both office and the Adam style. But this went only so

Croft-Murray, *Decorative Painting in England* 2 vols., (London, 1970) I, p. 317. For Robert Naismith, died 1793, see Howard Colvin, *A Bibliographical Dictionary of British Architects* (London, 1978) pp. 585–6.

[51] For Richardson see, Colvin, *Dictionary*, p. 687. After 1770, there are no ledger payments to Richardson and that for 1770 itself was small – £16–13–4.

[52] For Sacco see, Fleming, *Robert Adam*, p. 373, and Drummond's Bank, 1765 and 1766 ledgers, ff. 352, verso; 319, verso.

[53] Little seems to be known about J. P. Laurent apart from the Drummond ledger payments, 1768, ff. 319–20.

[54] See, Meadows, *Joseph Bonomi*, p. 6. There is a gap in payments to him at Drummond's after 1771 and until 1782. The last entry is for £18 in April, 1783.

[55] Calas appeared with Sacco in the ledger for 1765 and was paid £30. Legrix and Celeneux occur in 1766 but had disappeared by 1769; Delivet seems to have lasted only for 1768. All were paid around £20.

[56] For Manocchi see, Colvin, *Dictionary*, p. 537 and note 73; for Zucchi, Croft-Murray, *Decorative Painting*, II, pp. 296–300. Zucchi was successful enough to rent an Adam house in John Street in The Adelphi, Blair Adam Muniments, 4/21.

[57] Drummond's ledgers: the last recorded payment in them was for £100 in January, 1776.

far, and the contemporary diarist Joseph Farington made clear the difference between 'a draughtsman of buildings' and an architect. Zucchi's sphere was the wider, and extended from arabesque decoration to the iconographical figures in Adam's roundels and panels. Adam's confidence in him was sufficient to choose him to make the frontispiece for *The Works* itself, though, no doubt, the allegory he showed there was of Adam's devising (figure 71). Manocchi's contribution was colour – and strong colour at that. Such specialist associations were by no means uncommon; Cipriani had an early involvement with William Chambers' office, as did Peter Borgnis with the later Adam office.[58]

This is probably about as much as can be safely extracted from the Drummond accounts. They become in the later years as fragmentary and confused as the Adam practice itself, distorted by the brothers' constant speculative concerns. Such risky affairs embraced the office draughtsmen as well. The two principal ones associated with the office during the last decade of the 1780s – Daniel Robertson and Robert Morison – were deeply involved with the entrepreneurial aspect of the practice as was John Robertson the office clerk.[59] The whole situation was ably summed up by Bonomi who wrote that as early as the 1770s the 'building of the Adelphi and other undertakings of their own, made them neglect the work of others'. No doubt this explained the setting up in 1772 of the William Adam and Co. account at Drummond's in parallel with the original Adam one. The decline and shrinking of the Adelphi office throughout the eighties meant the abandonment of the didactic role of the drawing room which had been an essential part of the office's character from its inception at Lower Grosvenor Street. The Adelphi house had been given up in 1784 as 'larger than we find necessary' and the ultimate regime at 13, Albemarle Street in the 1790s was virtually a return to the hand to mouth existence of 1760.[60] The stark situation was frankly acknowledged in a letter from Robert Adam in 1785, where he apologised for delay, saying that the 'truth is that my principal Draughtsman who had these drawings in hand, was taken dangerously ill . . . But as the poor fellow keeps in a very lingering & precarious state of health, I am getting them done by another who is both more tedious & less capable.'[61] Such a letter would strongly suggest an office of perhaps not more than two or three, which in 1792 possibly shrank to the

[58] For Cipriani, see Harris, *Sir William Chambers*, p. 381; for Borgnis see Croft-Murray, *Decorative Painting*, II, p. 174 and Drummonds ledgers for 1784–9.

[59] For a summary of the careers of both Morison and Robertson see Colvin, *Dictionary*, pp. 557, 697–8. There are substantial payments to Daniel Robertson in the accounts of William Adam & Co. at Drummonds for 1782 and 1783. For John Robertson see, Colvin, *Dictionary*, p. 698.

[60] Blair Adam Muniments, 4/111; for an account of the various houses leased by the Adam office in The Adelphi see, *Survey of London, The Strand*, 18 (London, 1937) pp. 105, 110, 118, 136–7.

[61] National Library of Scotland MS 20500 f. 1.

Figure 71 Antonio Zucchi,
'A student conducted to
Minerva who points to
Greece and Italy'

draughtsman-clerk John Robertson alone. He was instructed on Adam's death,
'to collect and take charge of the Plans of every kind' and 'to direct what is
required', perhaps because there was no one else to do so.[62] While Adam
obviously had writing clerks, the administration and direction of the firm was
apparently carried on by him alone. His sister rather acidly described James
Adam's independence in 1792, and how it was necessary to have him briefed by
John Robertson on 'the different articles of business which Jamie is a stranger to
as he lived so much in the country & had not an opportunity of knowing much

[62] SRO GD 18/4974/1/24.

91

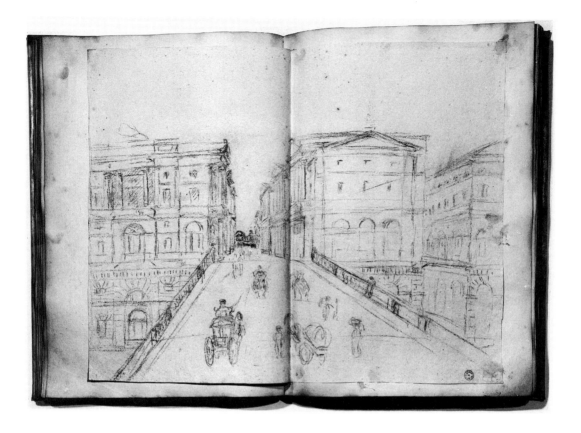

Figure 72 Robert Adam,
*Sketch perspective for the South
Bridge, Edinburgh*

of what was doing in the architecture part of the business'.[63] She also reckoned with touching optimism that Robertson and her two brothers, James and William, 'are equal to finish the works projected & already begun'.[64]

All of these draughtsmen worked within the restraints of the Adam office and their talents were further confined by the stylistic conventions of architectural drawing in the later eighteenth century. Adam also expected a degree of uniformity from his assistants and encouraged them to 'become equal to his Neighbours', though this might be interpreted as meaning to rise but not excel. There were probably exceptions. In the late office, both Morison and the Robertsons were permitted relative freedom in working up Adam's sketch drawings, on the assumption that they knew how the drawing should be developed, could understand his visual shorthand and accepted that the final drawing was always Adam's.[65] It did not always work. In the case of the

[63] *Ibid.*, GD 18/4961/40.
[64] *Ibid.*, GD 18/4974/1/24.
[65] For Robertson's drawings for John Adam see, Tait, *Robert Adam at Home*, p. 16. Several of these drawings are signed by both Adam and Robertson and though none is dated they are likely to

Figure 73   Robert Morison, 'Perspective view of the Buildings on the South Bridge, Edinburgh'

Edinburgh bridges scheme, Adam's rough but vigorous pencil sketch was handed over to Morison who produced a lacklustre wash perspective with poor architectural detailing and stock office figures and animals (figures 72 and 73). While it is possible to distinguish certain periods or cycles within the office, as for instance with the small-scale record drawings of the 1780s, the firm identification of hands can only be an uncertain business. At the start and close of the office, such attributions were easier, simply because the draughtsmen were few. Daniel Robertson's career in the declining years of the office, was typical in its versatility. He moved from working as John Adam's Edinburgh draughtsman to running the shrunken London office for Robert and James and, ultimately, the speculative ventures of William Adam. His handsome and smooth drawing style, with its adept use of watercolour and Robert Morison's scratchy, almost furtive, hand were characteristic of the declining office in the late 1780s (figures 74 and 75). It was this lack of consistency and apparent haste, typical of Morison, that appeared, too, in James Adam's office drawings after his return to the fray in 1792. His (or more likely Morison's) wash of 1794 for a lodge for the Duke of Buccleuch seemed almost slovenly when looked at beside Robertson's one for Blair Adam. In contrast, the simple watercolours and clear balanced drawings of Robert Adam in the late fifties seem to have belonged to a different age. The rapid expansion of the office after the return of James and

be of around 1780. The Adam office drawings for Brasted and Kirkdale of 1784 and 1786 are quite probably in Robertson's hand. (Soane Museum, AV LI, ff. 49–51; AV XXV 35, f. 52.) For Morison, see especially Andrew Fraser, *The Building of the Old College* (Edinburgh, 1990) pp. 133–5; and the rather scrappy drawings of Soane Museum AV XX, ff. 221–50.

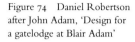

Figure 74 Daniel Robertson
after John Adam, 'Design for
a gatelodge at Blair Adam'

his band of *émigré* artists in 1763, meant that the tying of a hand to a particular
name became almost impossible. The thoroughly professional drawings by
Brunias for stucco and arabesque work at Kedleston of around 1760, were
indistinguishable four years later from a group of similarly accomplished but
anonymous hands. The format changed at this time too, and the black ink
margins, block lettering, elaborate scales and combined plan and wall elevations,
all characteristic of the Scottish office 'Baths' and the 'callants' of 1758, were
firmly abandoned by the London office after James Adam's return (figure 76).
The turning point in the office style seems to have been around 1764 when the
drawings achieved a remarkable consistency at all levels – working drawing,
section and elevation – with a carefully graded scale of decoration and colour.
Giuseppe Manocchi played a vital part in such a leap forward by convincing the
Adam brothers of the near primacy of colour for an Adam style.

As in so many of his architectural opinions, Adam stood apart from orthodox
neoclassical notions about colour. To Italian functionalists like Lodoli and his
followers, colour developed from the nature of building material or was limited
to a Palladian scheme of grey and white. Though he had read Winckelmann at
some time, Adam was consciously opposed to the theories on colour (or lack of
it) given in his *History of Ancient Art*, of 1764, where Winckelmann claimed that
colour at best 'assists beauty; generally, it heightens beauty and its forms but it
does not constitute it'.[66] Winckelmann expanded his principle further and more

---

[66] J. J. Winckelmann, *History of Ancient Art among the Greeks*, trans. G. H. Lodge (London, 1850),
p. 118.

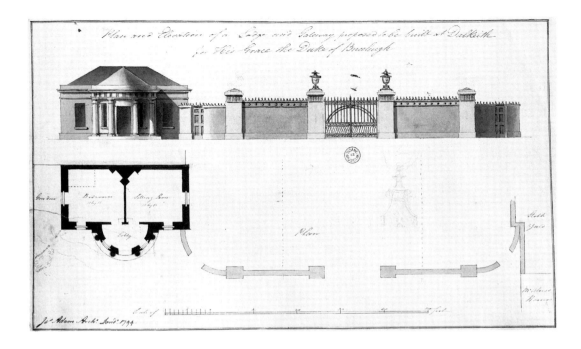

positively writing that 'colour, however, should have but little share in our consideration of beauty, because the essence of beauty consists, not in colour but in shape, and on this point enlightened minds will at once agree as white is the colour which reflects the greatest number of rays of light, and consequently is the most easily perceived, a beautiful body, will, accordingly, be more beautiful the whiter it is'.[67] Such a view cut remarkably little ice with Adam, and Winckelmann's comment on white was directly contradicted in *The Works* where Adam remarked on its 'crudeness'. James Adam found too the contemporary whitewashed ceiling of the Pantheon to be 'the most disadvantagous colour'. Instead, Adam saw colour as an essential part of Italian art and considered that its 'large masses of light and shade', added to the splendour and éclat of the general effect, and this was as true of watercolour as painting.[68]

Colour and its use in antiquity posed several problems for Adam and his draughtsmen. Little survived of the original colour patterns in the conventional sites that he and James Adam had seen in Italy, apart from the new discoveries they knew of at Pompeii and Herculaneum. Certainly they had looked at the ruins hard enough and with sufficient imagination to stimulate what Robert Adam, following Piranesi, termed his Etruscan style, whose shades were derived in a composite fashion from the mosaics and vases in the coloured volumes of

Figure 75 Robert Morison after James Adam, 'Plan and Elevation of a Lodge and Gateway proposed to be built at Dalkeith'

67 *Ibid.*   68 *The Works*, I, part IV, p. unnumbered.

Figure 76   Robert Adam,
'Plans and elevation of a
Rusticated Temple designed
for Mount-Stair'

Figure 77 Agostino Brunias after Robert Adam, *Interior elevation of the Painted Breakfast Room at Kedleston*

Sir William Hamilton's *Collection of Etruscan, Greek, and Roman Antiquities* of 1766/7. This was confirmed by James Adam who smugly thought it a 'much higher pleasure to examine them on the spot than in any book'.[69] But the integration of the strong colouring of the vases with their black and dark red backgrounds with the Adam style owed much to Manocchi's appearance in the office in 1765. Such a taste contrasted sharply with the bright colour schemes developed by Brunias that Adam had admired and written about so enthusiastically. He told James Adam that the painted breakfast room at Kedleston was 'quite in a new taste & I have Brunias now employed in painting in size to learn that method as oyl colours will by no means answer. They call that manner of painting in French, à la detrempe, and I think he succeeds wonderfully with it.'[70] The effect achieved there, was probably by some form of dragging which gave a lighter, less hard tone and a more regular surface than oil painting (figure 77, plate 2). If nothing else, this room showed Adam's and Brunias' understanding of the importance of colour and their readiness to experiment. However, it was obvious, too, that much of the appeal for Adam of this and other techniques was because they were new and foreign.

Manocchi made a large number of highly finished and coloured drawings for Adam. A few can be directly attributed to him and related to a particular

[69] *Library of The Fine Arts*, II, p. 237: and see lot 100 in the 1818 Adam sale (Bolton, *Architecture*, II, p. 331).
[70] Harris, *Robert Adam and Kedleston*, p. 52.

commission.[71] Some bear an almost hidden signature (forbidden by Robert Adam), others, such as a panel design for Luton of 1770 and a ceiling in Arlington Street of the following year, have colours annotated in Italian and so were probably his work (figure 78).[72] His drawings were usually rectangular with coloured borders and were just as likely to be for carpets or inlaid table tops (or in Italy vestments), as for ceilings or wall panels (figure 79). The scale was the same, as were the run of background colours done in gouache rather than Brunias' familiar watercolour, pale green, pink, yellow and Pompeian red. Against them, were set much darker shades, such as blue or red with rosettes and arabesques often painted in old gold. In all of these, and to a lesser extent in Manocchi's grotesque panels, the style was a neat and exact one, well suited to the repetitive form of the compositions and more precise than other office hands at this time. Indeed, he was judged in Rome, in 1773, to have a great facility through long practice in his 'arabese ornaments', but not for accuracy or a fine touch.[73] What Manocchi's colleagues made of Adam's latest protégé is hard to say. No doubt, they were encouraged by the familiar Adam refrain 'to become equal to his Neighbours', and many seem to have risen to the challenge. His influence was probably apparent in the strong contrasts and rich, dark base colours found in the ceiling designs proposed in the seventies for the Drury Lane Theatre or the interior of Mistley, and certainly in the Etruscan schemes for Derby House and Osterley (figure 80, plate 3). Its final form was later still in Bonomi's independent work at Packington Hall in 1787.[74] Though Manocchi's colours may have flourished in the office, he did not. He returned disgruntled to Italy in 1773. His signature on a handful of drawings, was possibly enough to have unsettled the sensitive Adam brothers who held strong and unreasonable views on the ownership of drawings. Though they claimed that 'we have not trod the path of others, nor derived aid from their labours', such sentiments did not apply to the drawing offices in Grosvenor Street or The Adelphi or to the output of Manocchi, Bonomi, Richardson and other mechanics to the Adam

[71] For Manocchi, see Damie Stillman, *Decorative Work of Robert Adam*, (London, 1966) pp. 42–3; Colvin, *Dictionary*, p. 537; and *Italienische Zeichnungen der Kunstbibliothek*, (Berlin, 1975) pp. 214–15. The bulk of the drawings in Soane Museum, AV XXI, XV and XVI are designs by him for ceilings, table tops and carpets.

[72] Soane Museum, AV XII, XVI, XX contain drawings dated 1765 and 1766 and AV XII, ff. 74, 76, some dated 1770 and 1771. Manocchi returned to Italy in 1773 and 'considered himself badly treated'. (Meadows, *Joseph Bonomi*, p. 5.)

[73] The English Jesuit in Rome, Father John Thorpe knew Manocchi, repeated too that 'he was treated very ungenerously by the Adamses', and that they owed 'their credit in arabese ornaments' to him. (Father Thorpe correspondence, 1768–91, Ugbrooke Park.)

[74] For Drury Lane see Soane Museum AV XIV, f. 16 and Mistley f. 29. Adam's Etruscan style is discussed in Stillman, *Decorative Work of Robert Adam*, pp. 22, 36–8; and Damie Stillman, 'Robert Adam and Piranesi', *Essays Presented to Rudolf Wittkower*, 2 vols., (London, 1967), I, pp. 203–4; and for Packington see, Meadows, *Joseph Bonomi*, pp. 20–1.

Figure 78   Giuseppe
Manocchi, *Grotesque panel*

Figure 79   Giuseppe
Manocchi, *Design for a floor
covering*

Figure 80 Adam Office,
'Sketch for a Coloured
Ceiling', Drury Lane Theatre

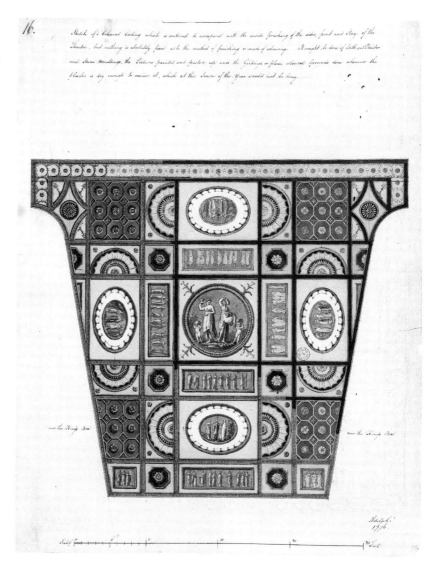

machine. In the office, a hurried pencil sketch to be worked up, sometimes with colours noted, was enough for Adam to claim ownership and control over this or any further drawings.

Manocchi offered a new insight into the way colour could be effectively used, and this may have more obliquely influenced Adam than his office. His picturesque washes and watercolours, which were revived in the mid-seventies, showed a concern with sombre shades and broken colours that was very different from the light tones of his Italian drawings of the fifties or, for that matter, the strident, full-blooded colours of Manocchi. The new theories and

Figure 81 George
Richardson after Robert
Adam, 'Lady Home's
Staircase'

power of colour were fully recognised by Robert Adam, absorbed and turned
in characteristic fashion to his own ends. This allowed him to convert even
black and white into a variety of tones. In his architectural drawings, and
particularly those by Bonomi, the shadow assumed greater importance and
suggested a mood as much as a colour. This was outstandingly so, in Adam's
own tinted works. In the section through the staircase hall, at Home House
(figure 81), or in Richardson's drawing for the revised design of the Marble Hall
at Kedleston, such shadows were used with sensitivity, and subtly merged and
muted the colour schemes and spaces. Something of this can be seen, too, in the

interior engravings of *The Works* where hatching was applied to suggest light, depth and movement. This increasing concern with mood marked the book as a turning point in the Adam practice. Without doubt, *The Works* summarised the strength of the brothers' experience in Italy and the successful style modelled upon it. But it was, too, a book that saw such an achievement in past terms and hinted at a new style waiting to be fashioned in the wings.

4

The Works

THE LAST AND, possibly, most superficial legacy of the brothers' Italian tours and the drawings that they made during them, was their book on the ruins of Diocletian's palace at Split, then part of the Venetian empire. It was originally conceived as a piece of architectural and antiquarian scholarship where the author showed taste and learning in equal measure, with an exotic dash of travel knowledge. It had a chequered evolution beginning as a new Desgodetz, then as work on the 'Baths' correcting Palladio, then Hadrian's Villa, then as the antiquities of Pola. In the end, it hung as a modified millstone round Robert Adam's neck. Apart from its promotional role, it had as its theme the importance and standards of Roman private architecture. This was a neglected topic that partly-justified the Adam country-house practice and gave a theoretical validity to the Adam style. It was a theme that Adam returned to in *The Works*, almost a decade later. The two books – *The Ruins* of 1764 and *The Works* of 1773 onwards – mark together the rise and dominance of the Adam style, first as a striking form of eclectic classicism and then, after 1774, as a manifestation of the picturesque. Both books relied heavily on illustration to set out an argument taken up and vigorously pursued in the text. It was the skilful interplay of the two in *The Works* – itself an aspect of the picturesque – that gave the book its decisive role in the later years of the Adam practice.

Though these two books were produced with different ends in mind, there can be little doubt that *The Works* was of greater importance. It was more modern than *The Ruins* which relied heavily on a familiar mix of archaeological and historical learning leavened with a series of magnificent prints, master-minded by Clérisseau and Zucchi. The opening panorama of Split set the pace (figure 82). For better or worse, it belonged to a literary tradition which can be traced back to Fynes Moryson's travelogue of Italy, *An Itinerary*, at the end of the sixteenth century.[1] There was quite a different past for *The Works*, which

---

[1] For the evolution of *The Ruins* see, Eileen Harris, *British Architectural Books and Writers* (Cambridge, 1990), pp. 76–83.

103

revived the miscellaneous mixture of architecture and decoration last seen effectively in the late sixteenth-century pattern books. The key here was a pictorial approach which explored a building by letting it unfold through a variety of deep perspectives and flat elevations. *The Works* offered at a variety of levels an essential analysis of the Adam style as it had evolved during the decade of the sixties. At the same time, it managed a subtle change of emphasis where the picturesque was unveiled as an essential part of the endlessly flexible Adam style.

Nothing perhaps made clearer the dominance of drawing over word than the farming out of the text for *The Ruins* to the Edinburgh cousin and historian William Robertson, whose part as a shadow rather than ghost was similar to Clérisseau's.[2] In a sense it was an expression of failure. The manuscript written before November, 1757, and presumably by Robert, was historical and factual with little or none of the analytical sharpness of Robertson's work. Called 'Reasons and Motives for Undertaking the Voyage to Spalatro in Dalmatia', it was cast in two parts, the first giving a description of Spalatro, the surrounding country and a chronology of the Adam expedition; the second was a social and political account of Dalmatia.[3] Neither part dealt with the palace in any great detail and the whole was similar to Wood and Dawkins' accounts of the *Ruins of Palmyra* of 1753, and the *Ruins of Balbec* of 1757. Wood's description of his 'Journey from Palmyra to Balbec' was clearly in Adam's mind when he explained that 'in this I have followed the Example of Gentlemen who have already given to the public two most learned and perfect works'.[4] In the rejected manuscript, the architectural element was limited to a description of the plates and the plates themselves. To employ them as illustrations to the argument of the text was essentially Robertson's idea for he, as a historical writer, knew how to sustain and advance a set of opinions by examples. It says much for Adam's judgement that he was willing to scrap one for the other and to abandon entirely his original notion of 'giving a history of the place, its commerce and inhabitants, likewise some sketch of the life of Diocletian'.[5] Yet he remained in control. He had the odd reservation about the text as too strong and was sad to see his account of the troubles with the Venetian governor truncated, 'though I dont say that Willie has done right to curtail them'.

There was no such ghost for *The Works* and the literary part anyhow remained very much in Adam hands and particularly those of James. Whatever were his short-comings as an author – long-winded and unpunctual – he was,

[2] John Fleming, 'An Adam Miscellany: The Journey to Spalatro', *Architectural Review*, 123 (February, 1958), pp. 103–7.
[3] SRO GD 18/4953.
[4] *The Ruins*, p. 1.   [5] SRO GD 18/4953 f. 23.

Figure 82 'View of the
Town of Spalatro from the
South West'

in his brother's eyes, a spirit 'with that love and enthusiasm of architecture, which no one could feel that has not formed very extensive ideas of it'.[6] This certainly came across strongly, in the more sustained of the various prefaces, that constituted the text for *The Works*. So much so, that in their density and spirited argument they existed almost as an end in themselves, only brought to earth by the accompanying prints. Such ambiguity lay at the heart of the entire book, for unlike *The Ruins*, it had no ready-made story to tell easily and elegantly. Instead it was a hybrid: a series of brilliant but unequal and loosely connected parts which in some ways gave an episodic and evolving account of the Adam style. But like all hybrids, it showed a vigour and magnificence that put its genetic rivals in the shade. Largely to blame for this editorial eccentricity was James Adam's original scheme for *The Works* as a picture book from which the individual plates could be extracted and used to decorate the then fashionable print room. Such a notion went back to 1762 and his British Museum project, where prints of English antiquities were to be sold in volumes of fifty plates, at £50 a piece.[7] A year later, he thought these could be done easily and speedily by his Veronese, presumably the draughtsman Giuseppe Sacco, who was 'perfectly clever in this style'. Such thinking may partly explain the strong visual character of *The Works* at the outset, where the changing viewpoint of the different plates was exploited to give the maximum variety and drama. The steep perspective given of the garden front at Kenwood where architecture, garden building and landscape were cleverly balanced, was conspicuously different from the familiar flat elevation used for the plates of Luton or the Carlton House screen (figure 83). It needed little imagination to

[6] A. F. Tytler (ed.) *Memoirs of the Life and Writings of the Honourable Henry Home of Kames, Supplement* (Edinburgh, 1809), p. 54.
[7] SRO GD 18/4945.

Figure 83   'View of the
south Front of the Villa at
Kenwood'

see how effective these and other prints from *The Works*, such as those for clocks
and lamps, would be in the run-of-the-mill domestic print room or gallery
(figure 84). There existed also at the back of James Adam's mind his putative
'history of architecture' which, though it survived in bits and pieces, was
nevertheless a piece of architectural theory of which James at least was proud.
To run the two enterprises together successfully and rapidly as a strongly
propagandist book was a typical Adam dream in which their genius would be
made as obvious as their critics and rivals confounded. That *The Works* for all its
fragmentary nature came close to this, was proof of both Adam resilience and
brilliance. *The Works* was, in financial terms, a failure and obviously so, in the
almost threadbare character of its later numbers in which the prefaces dwindled
to the point where there was ultimately no text of any consequence.[8] Such
a falling-off in spirit may well have undermined confidence in much of what
was said and shown, but it would be unfair to judge so remarkable a book on
commercial terms alone.

   The shadow of two books lay heavily upon both *The Ruins* and *The Works*.
This pall was formed by what might be termed the ancestral *Vitruvius Scoticus*,
and more deeply by James Stuart's *Antiquities of Athens*, of 1762. *Vitruvius
Scoticus* as a bald collection of architectural engravings had been underway in
1727 and after William Adam's death, it was taken up again by John Adam. For

[8] Harris, *Architectural Books*, p. 88.

Figure 84 'Various Pieces of Ornamental Furniture'

all that, it only appeared in print in 1812 under the aegis of William Adam, the youngest of all the Adam brothers.[9] Small attempt was made in it, to disguise the book's origins as little more than a visual record of William Adam's buildings, made to popularise both author and style. It had now been expanded to include

[9] See William Adam, *Vitruvius Scoticus*, ed. James Simpson (Edinburgh, 1980), pp. 6–9.

the early Scottish works of his sons, especially John, whose staid, gothic castle at Douglas was possibly the imaginative highlight of a limited architectural career (figure 85).[10] *Vitruvius Scoticus* lacked any literary element and was probably never intended to have had one. It was simply a visual account of an architectural practice which had by 1812 become an anachronism and irrelevant piece of hagiography. But in a deeper and more complicated way, it acted as a sort of catalyst for Robert Adam, which encouraged him to succeed where his father had failed. Both he and James Adam had their books published with reasonable speed and outdid *Vitruvius Scoticus* too, in the excellence of their prints and the impact of the text. On the other hand, Stuart's *Antiquities of Athens* provided a different sort of spur. The brothers had been prepared for it since 1757, when Robert wrote that 'we all know how much the very fame of it blasted the reputations of those works of Pa & B-k', nonetheless its actual appearance was a shock, 'I can't say I like this sort of forestalling much'.[11] What troubled Adam about the *Antiquities of Athens* was that it offered a similar and just as detailed analysis of neglected monuments as *The Ruins*, with the additional twist that Stuart's *Proposal* of 1751 had promised three, and later four, volumes.[12] Worse still, it had much the same emphasis on the visual and like *The Ruins* had developed the perspective view to give atmosphere to the architectural setting, several of which were more attractive than Clérisseau's drawings of Spalatro (figure 86). However, the introduction, which had been written with the Wood and Dawkins publications in mind, could just as easily be seen as a defence against Stuart. Adam had made the sharp point through William Robertson that while, 'the remains of a single Palace' could not vie with 'those surprising and almost unknown monuments of sequestered grandeur', his book alone contained 'the only full and accurate Designs that have hitherto been published of any private Edifice of the Ancients'.[13] While this was not strictly true, Adam was innovative in his scrutiny of the private architecture of antiquity, a subject more or less ignored by Stuart and others.

The Antiquities of Athens avoided a great deal of the travelogue character of Palmyra and Balbeck and concentrated instead on the buildings rather than the civilisation which built them. After the dedication to the King, there followed a preface with extensive footnotes, many of which were in Greek, as much to establish the book's scholarly credentials as anything else. The clear theme of the preface was the justification of the book – that 'Greece was the great Mistress of the Arts and Rome, in this respect, no more than her disciple'.[14] Stuart

---

[10] *Ibid.*, p. 21.   [11] Fleming, *Adam Miscellany*, p. 107.
[12] Harris, *Architectural Books*, pp. 440–1.   [13] *The Ruins*, p. 1.
[14] James Stuart, *The Antiquities of Athens* (London, 1762), p. 1; for a stylistic account of the book see, David Watkin, *Athenian Stuart* (London, 1982), pp. 13–22.

Figure 85 'West Front of
Douglas Castle'

*West Front of DOUGLAS CASTLE The Seat of
His Grace the Duke of Douglas in the County of Lanark.*

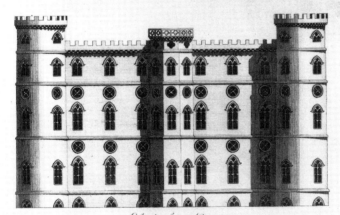

Elevation of one end

East Front

109

Figure 86 Frontispiece from
Antiquities of Athens (1762)

maintained that 'all the most admired Buildings which adorned the Imperial City, were but imitations of Greek Originals', and moreover, architecture since the renaissance had been reduced and restrained within narrow limits by the examples found in Italy.[15] The standing in such a hierarchy of a provincial fourth-century palace like Diocletian's cannot have been high. That Adam saw it as a representative of the forgotten class of private architecture was neither here nor there, for to Stuart it was simply a distant copy of a Greek villa. In the rest of the book, Stuart arranged the various prints of the individual monuments as separate sections, internally numbered and introduced by a long description and history. It was a lesson Adam learnt for *The Works*, for, amongst the Adam drawings, there were at least two copies after Stuart's plates of the Doric Portico in Athens, probably taken from the presentation copy in his library (figure 87). The idea of a short sequence of plates had clearly rubbed off in *The Works* itself where the first two parts, devoted to Syon and Kenwood, opened with a visually stunning sequence of plates which smoothly moved the reader from the outside landscape to the interior of the house. Such an arrangement more or less beat Stuart at his own game and in the process, gave meaning to the basic Adam concepts of movement and variety.

The Works was obviously intended as a summation of the Adam career as far as 1773. Its appearance at that time may well have been fired by the inclusion of Adam buildings in the 1767 and 1771 volumes of *Vitruvius Britannicus*. Adam was

---

[15] Stuart, *ibid*.

Figure 87 Adam Office,
Copy of plate I from
Antiquities of Athens

elliptically referred to in the text as well, and one of the authors, James Gandon, castigated the Adam style as little more than as 'rummaging even the dung-hills of antiquity'.[16] The brothers no doubt felt it was time for their version of what they had achieved. Paradoxically in what was essentially a retrospective book, *The Works* looked forward and offered the picturesque as the key to the next twenty years or so. Something of this was explained in the several prefaces that introduced different parts of the book and was apparent graphically in the style of the plates themselves with their obvious debt to Piranesi's balanced asymmetry and variety. The fact that some of the plates could be bought coloured clearly, underscored its evolving nature and the continual search by its authors for variety and novelty, terms they themselves had used in their first preface. To them should be added accuracy, for the preface made clear that these specially coloured plates repeated 'the tints, used in the execution' and the overall effect was part of 'our national style of ornament'.[17] In this way and at

[16] Harris, *Architectural Books*, p. 203.   [17] *The Works*, I, part I, p. 7.

several levels, *The Works* offered an understanding of the picturesque drawings and watercolours which Robert Adam developed during the late seventies and eighties.

Several direct precursors can be found for at least six of *The Works'* prefaces. The most direct was that of 1776, on the history of private and public architecture, which was certainly derived from the introduction to *The Ruins*. To a degree, too, the essay on classicism which introduced that of 1774, was culled from Adam's letter to Lord Kames on the classical orders, of 1763 itself based on James Adam's opinions.[18] The preface on the Etruscan style from volume II of 1779, was inspired both by Piranesi's *Della Magnificenza* and more particularly by Allan Ramsay's *Dialogue on Taste*, of 1755, though typically neither was mentioned in a long footnote on current Etruscan studies.[19] Compounding the heterogeneous character of such introductory essays was James Adam's unfinished history of architecture, underway in 1762 at Rome, and his more complex history of taste of the same time.[20] The most obvious connection between these and *The Works* was the first preface of 1773 where the picturesque element was an adaptation of parts of the Roman essays. His opinion had changed little then as now, 'What is so material in excellence in Landscip is not less requisite for Composition in Architecture, namely the variety of the Contours or rise & fall of the different parts', was adapted with little change to footnote A of the first preface.[21] This and the other prefaces, all varied in length, style and purpose. They were as much a partnership between the brothers as between text and plates. In fact, the prefaces were largely James Adam's handiwork, overseen by Robert Adam, who also contributed the description of the plates themselves.

Much of what James Adam had written in Rome was not his own work. He was strongly influenced by his advisers, particularly Piranesi, who was at this time attempting to order his own architectural theories for publication. He had published his *Della Magnificenza* before 1762 but it was the rather more original *Parere* of 1765, that inspired many of Adam's more imaginative ideas about variety and ornament. The proof for much of this intellectual pudding may well have been gradually apparent in Piranesi's work at the Piazza and church of Santa Maria del Priorato, of which the office had at least three incomplete copy drawings – two of the church and one of the stables – which were probably

[18] Tytler, *Kames Supplement*, pp. 50–5.

[19] *The Works*, II, part I, p. unnumbered. Adam wrote that, 'we have consulted Monfaucon, Count Caylus, Count Passeri, Father Gori, and the whole collection of antiquarians'. He also referred to 'Dempster, de Etrur Regal. Cluverius, ital. Antiq. the Marquis Scipio Massei, and Francesco Mariani'.

[20] See p. 64.

[21] SRO GD 18/4954, f. 5, and *The Works*, I, part I, p. 3. See too Fleming, *Robert Adam*, p. 315.

made for James Adam in 1762 (figure 58).[22] Certainly neither of the Adam brothers would have ignored *Della Magnificenza*, for it contained, if nothing else, a congenial attack on Allan Ramsay's *Dialogue on Taste*.[23] Both the brothers sided with Piranesi in maintaining the supremacy of Roman over Greek classicism and its freedom from most forms of doctrinaire restraint. His airing, there, and before in *Le antichità Romane* of 1756 of the problem of public architecture was again music to the Adam ears. Both such hobby horses were ridden boldly and afresh in the other prefaces to *The Works*. Particularly exasperating for Adam however, was the position held by Chambers' *Designs of Chinese Buildings* as the English counterpart of Piranesi. This book, which appeared in 1757, contained a fair degree of sympathy for the importance of variety and novelty, though, in this case, it was limited to Chinese art and architecture. Chambers also claimed that Chinese artists readily appreciated the importance of association and the powerful effect of contrast on the sensitive mind and the similar evocative powers of form, colour and shades.[24] James Adam's similar reflections on sentiment or association, probably inspired like Chambers' by Dubos' *Réflexions critiques*, were different in that they had Italian rather than Chinese landscape artists in mind. A favourite Adam painter like Zuccarelli could be relied upon in this fashion, to supply his canvases with the necessary 'agreeable and diversified contour, that groups and contrasts like a picture', which the 1773 preface of *The Works* equated with architectural composition.[25] This was a gentler version of the picturesque, more restrained than the often contrived theatricality of Salvator Rosa and Marco Ricci, and one that appealed especially to the English taste. James Adam's view that 'they who study after nature take the evening or the morning when the sun is low and the shadows are broad', was one he shared with his brother whose tinted landscapes reflected just that position.[26]

It should be emphasised that there were differences between the 1762 essay and similar parts that appeared in the preface to *The Works*. The words and phrases they had in common were misleading, for the two treatises served quite different purposes. The essay of 1762 was probably meant as a commentary and explanation of James Adam's ambitious Parliament scheme whereas the preface of a decade later was a broad, almost rambling account of architectural terms and their use by the brothers. It lacked the constant refrain of variety and novelty apparent in the earlier essay, which had itself (perhaps unduly) benefited from

---

[22] See pp. 67–9.
[23] See, Wilton-Ely, *Piranesi*, p. 67.
[24] William Chambers, *Designs of Chinese Buildings*, (London, 1757), p. ii.
[25] Fleming, *Robert Adam*, pp. 256, 270; *The Works*, I, part I, p. 3.
[26] Fleming, *Robert Adam*, p. 315.

James Adam's exposure to Piranesi's theories on the inventive power of ornament. While the message of the importance of movement was couched in the same landscape terms of 'hill and dale' and 'light and shade', and the original sentence that 'an excellence in landscape is not less requisite for composition in architecture' was repeated in much the same form, the examples given for each differed significantly.[27] The original prototypes for the Adam form of movement, Blenheim and Heriot's Hospital, Edinburgh, were changed exclusively to Vanbrugh's Blenheim and Castle Howard, and St Peter's – which was both admired and criticised in the first essay – was praised along with Le Vau's Quatre Nations.[28] The last was possibly derived from a close reading of Laugier, *Essai sur l'architecture*, by one or other of the Adams. A further addition was a modest reference to the south front of Kedleston as a prime example of 'so much movement and contrast'.[29] Indeed, Kedleston was an ideal choice, for in a broad way, it matched extremely well the preface's equation of the vocabularies of architecture and painting to each other. Alongside Adam's work on the house and the various garden buildings, he supposedly had been briefed by Sir Nathaniel Curzon to landscape the park with the evocative 'hill and dale' of *The Works* glimpsed in the surviving plan and perspectives (figure 108).[30] It was a scheme that probably appealed to Curzon, whose taste, like Robert Adam's, ran to Zuccarelli's allegorical landscapes as well as seeing Derbyshire as the makeshift *campagna*.

The uncertain tone of the first preface was hardly surprising for it was at some stage substituted for an essay on the general history of architecture in Britain. This ultimately appeared later in 1778 as the fifth preface. The gloss given for this was that 'We intended to have prefixed to our designs a dissertation concerning the rise and progress of architecture in Great Britain.'[31] That this had been held over to what was termed a period of greater leisure probably meant that James Adam had not finished the text in time. Instead, there was the preface worked up from the 1762 manuscript, with laborious footnotes in emulation of James Stuart's. These covered not only movement but less interesting forms such as the entablature, tabernacle form, and the explanation of words like grotesque and *rainçeau*, much of which was *staffage* rather than technical definition. Its hidden purpose was, of course, to justify decoration for little of this had any particular relevance to the eight plates of Syon House which

[27] *Ibid.*

[28] *Ibid. The Works*, I, part 1, pp. 3–4. Laugier praised Quatre Nations for its 'elegant form and the graceful blending of the curved and straight lines of its plan', Herrmann, *Laugier*, pp. 29, 31.

[29] *The Works*, I, part 1, p. 3.

[30] Fleming, pp. 257–8 and Harris, *Adam and Kedleston*, pp. 74–5. Adam's 'Sketch for the Pleasure Garden' is discussed in Gervase Jackson-Stops, *An English Arcadia* (London, 1992), pp. 96–8.

[31] *The Works*, I, part 1, p. 6.

followed. Nor was the case greatly different, in the fifth preface where the belated history was attached to a miscellaneous group of plates which had only a royal provenance, in common. The character of this fifth part was perhaps intended to have been strengthened by the inclusion of James Adam's Parliament elevation, of 1763, alongside the related plate of the Britannic Order.[32]

The remarkable feature of the prefaces was that most of them made better sense independent of the plates they introduced. The first and fifth most obviously covered much the same ground and together explained how 'the peculiar distinction of the present reign' (fifth), and the 'late changes it [Architecture] has undergone' (first), and how this had all helped the Adam brothers to effect their kind of revolution. The fifth preface then continued where the first had left off, and attempted a definition of the Adam style. This was given clearly and forcibly by James Adam who wrote that the new manner had 'greater variety of form, greater beauty in design, greater gaiety and elegance of ornament', in the interior, while the outside 'composition is more simple, more grand, more varied in its contour, and imposes on the mind from the superior magnitude and movement of its parts'.[33] Such an emphasis on the simple, grand and various was a distant echo of James Adam's Roman manuscript. His section there, on the elevation and its movement rather enigmatically admired the distant view of a building because 'at a considerable distance we must of necessity lose all the graces of detail and decoration so that we have nothing remaining but the beauty of a well disposed variety of high and low projections and recesses'.[34] Such a concept of beauty later became one of the corner-stones of the Adam picturesque style.

The first part of *The Works* appeared in 1773 at what was a critical time in the Adam fortunes. The five parts that appeared together as volume II in 1779 marked a deepening crisis in their affairs which had, inevitably enough, affected the book itself. The slide in the book's fortunes was well documented, and in the 1821 Adam sale, 'large quantities' remained to be auctioned off for next to nothing.[35] As with their collection of Old Masters, the brothers had badly misjudged the market of the late seventies. So much so, that there was about the later parts of the second volume a desperate air of cut and run, where the issues became a ragbag of variable quality with the introductory essay eliminated and

---

[32] See p. 59.

[33] *The Works*, I, part v, p. unnumbered.

[34] Fleming, *Robert Adam*, p. 315.

[35] Bolton, *Architecture*, II, p. 336 and A. A. Tait, 'The Sale of Robert Adam's Drawings', *Burlington Magazine*, 120 (1978) p. 451.

the description shrunk to terse captions. These, in themselves, may explain James Adam's departure from the project and the office.[36]

The five prefaces which composed the first volume of 1778, all had a strong declamatory style, reminding the reader, with more evangelism than vanity, what the two brothers had achieved and at what cost. In reading the prefaces in this fashion, the brothers seem – almost deliberately – to have set their revolution in the past and cast themselves as key figures in a history of taste. Nothing perhaps made this clearer than their commentary of 1779 on the Countess of Derby's dressing room and its Etruscan decoration where 'if judges in architecture shall think any praise due to the discovery of another class of decoration and embellishment, they may know to whom the art is indebted for this improvement' (figure 88).[37] They further and rather brazenly explained that any person of taste would know that the Adam Etruscan style 'differs from any thing hitherto practised in Europe'. The obvious purpose of *The Works* had been to both define and defend the Adam style. The soul of their architecture lay in the seizure of 'the beautiful spirit of antiquity', and its infusion with novelty and variety. In this way, they were both attacking the strictness of the increasingly fashionable Greek style and justifying their enthusiasm for the equally fashionable picturesque whose essential elements were novelty, variety and antiquity in all its guises. The brothers' firm rejection in *The Works* of the Greek revival and all that it stood for, underlined their equally firm acceptance of the picturesque. In this way, *The Works* showed the Adam brothers – certainly Robert – nailing the colours of the picturesque to their mast as the mainsail for the imminent decade of the eighties.

The Adam disparagement of Greek architecture was more subtle than either that found in Piranesi's *Della Magnificenza* or Chambers' *Civil Architecture* of 1759. The 1774 preface of the second part of *The Works* was devoted to classicism and the Doric order and was perhaps the most detailed statement of the Adam position in this controversy. The preface was largely a reworking of a letter written earlier to Lord Kames, in which Robert Adam was cautious about any liberties, which he called 'a dangerous licence', taken with the classical orders.[38] A decade later, he had changed his mind and was prepared to experiment with even so absolute a classical force as the Doric capital to give it

---

36 Robert Adam's sister wrote in March, 1792, after his death that 'the different articles of business which Jamie is a stranger to as he lived so much in the country & had not an opportunity of knowing much of what was doing in the architecture part of the business' (SRO GD 18/4961/40). James Adam seems to have acquired an estate near Harlow, on the Essex–Hertfordshire border, around 1775–9 (Blair Adam Muniment, 1454/4). It was from this experience he wrote his *Practical Essays in Agriculture*.

37 *The Works*, II, part I, p. unnumbered.

38 Tytler, *Kames Supplement*, p. 55.

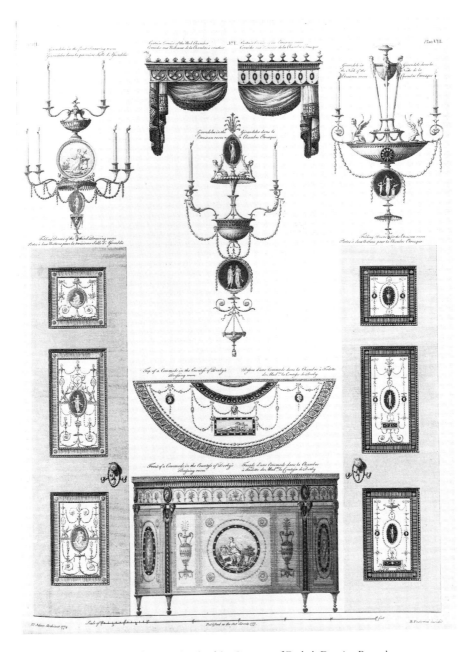

Figure 88   'Decorative and furniture details of the Countess of Derby's Dressing Room'

more grace and enrichment, much as he had done with the pilasters on the south front of Kenwood.[39] A similar sort of licence was used in the reworking in the early 1760s of Keene's Doric capitals on the Bowood portico.[40] All such experimentation or deviation from the classical norm as justified on the grounds of variety and as the irrefutable hallmark of the great artist. 'We must however beg leave to observe', the preface went, 'that we can see no reason for assigning to each order its precise entablature, fixed down unalterably both in figure and dimension. Different circumstances of situation and propriety ought to vary the form, and also the proportion, of all entablatures. A latitude in this respect, under the hand of an ingenious and able artist, is often productive of great novelty, variety, and beauty.'[41] In his plate of the garden bridge at Syon, from *The Works*, there was as much ridicule as variety in Adam's use of the Erechtheion caryatids as a risible variation on the three Graces, in the decoration of the bridge (figure 89). That Athenian Stuart had not included the remarkable Erechtheion portico in the *Antiquities of Athens* made it an even sharper joke.

The theme of the second preface that there were no absolute values in architecture, no 'immediate standards in nature', and that art had more to do with pleasing the eye than following any set of conventional rules. This was really little more than a simplification of Dubos' notion of sentiment as a sort of sixth sense. An outstanding example of this was the classical capital which, Adam maintained, could be adjusted visually with great success as had been done in the past by the ancients. In all such discussion, Adam made little or no distinction between Greek and Roman classicism and in fact, could be equally critical of both. Though he may have disliked the Greek Ionic volute as much too heavy, in his opinion the Roman version was little better.[42] He preferred, too, the sharpness of the Greek moulding to the Roman. In all of this, his attitude was essentially an eclectic one, as the capitals which he had devised for Kenwood, Syon and Bowood showed all too well. The Ionic and Doric ones he designed for Kenwood were not, as he made clear in *The Works*, subject to any precise or particular rule and behind such arguments was the thinly disguised conviction that the end justified the means.

There can be little doubt that both the driving force behind *The Works* and its technical direction, lay almost completely in the hands of the two brothers. Unlike *The Ruins*, there were no associates who had a ghostly role similar to that

---

[39] *The Works*, I, part II, p. 6.

[40] For Adam's eclectic use of the classical orders see, succinctly, J. M. Crook, *The Greek Revival* (London, 1972), pp. 72–3.

[41] *The Works*, I, part II, p. 7.

[42] Adam wrote that 'the volute of Grecian Ionic has always appeared to us by much too heavy, and those used by the Romans seem rather to border on the other extreme' (*Ibid.*, p. 5).

Figure 89 'Perspective View
of the Bridge at Syon'

of Robertson or Clérisseau. The theoretical positions taken, in the various
prefaces, were largely those of James and stretched back to his Roman days and
association with Piranesi, while the direction of the prints lay very much in
Robert Adam's capable hands. The surviving drawing for the engraving of the
furniture at Kenwood, of 1774, showed clearly how Adam went about the
business of setting up the plate which in this case was later engraved by Patrick
Begbie (figure 90). The pen and ink drawing was very much in the style of
Adam's earlier sketch for the setting up of his antiquities in Lower Grosvenor
Street and was composed with much the same regard for symmetry (figure 65).
The rough pencil measurements alongside the mirrors show the problems that
were encountered and only partially resolved in the plate itself, which was
arguably less successful compositionally than the drawing. The discarding of
the curtain cornice from Derby House in Grosvenor Square had led to a
corresponding exaggeration of the height of the glass in the great room at
Kenwood which dominated the centre of the page and left unresolved a
conspicuous void at the top left of the print (figure 91). In adjusting the size of
the furniture in this arbitrary fashion, Adam was true to his visual principles
where effect was much more important than accuracy. The drawing, too,
highlighted Adam's concern about a symmetry of unequal parts and here the
influence of Piranesi's engraved work was evident, particularly the furniture
plates from the *Diverse maniere d'adornare i cammini*, of 1769 (figure 92). Both

Figure 90 Robert Adam,
Sketch drawing for Plate VIII for
The Works

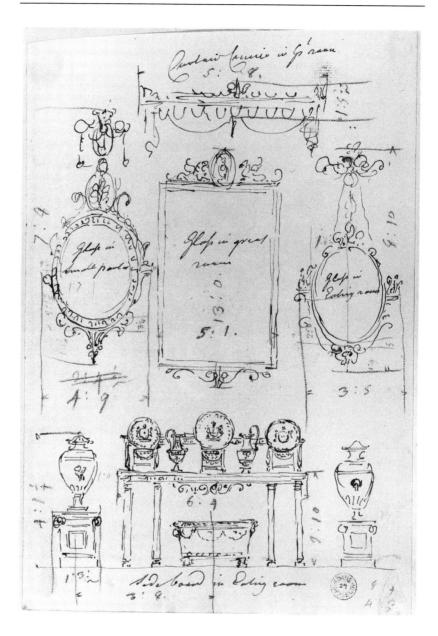

Adam and Piranesi were alive to the variety of contrasts that could be conjured up by such symmetry of the unlike, and exploited it to the maximum.

In the second volume of *The Works* which appeared in five parts in 1779, the fourth part was a continuation of the Adam work at Syon. In all, there are six plates of which four had been engraved by Piranesi after Adam drawings, dated 1761 and 1763. They were probably agreed before James Adam left Rome though he made no reference to such a project and there are no related

Figure 91 'Design for various pieces of furniture'

Figure 92 G. B. Piranesi, 'Quest'orologio A e stato estquito in metalle . . .'

drawings of that period to suggest any conspicuous level of cooperation. Only one of them, plate five, showed Piranesi and Adam arranging the plate of classical details as though they were a group of fragments from *Della Magnificenza* or the *Lapides Capitolini* (figure 93). Both composition and engraving may have been Piranesi's imaginative handwriting, and for this reason James Adam acknowledged the debt in his brief preface.[43] The five details that together composed the plate were set out asymmetrically with acute changes from flat elevation to profile giving depth and surprise, just as the sophisticated hatching suggested recession and highlights. The influence of such a plate can be detected in a similar one for the architectural details of Kenwood, of 1774, where the

---

43 *The Works*, II, part IV, p. unnumbered. With characteristic Adam disingenuousness, it was noted that some of Piranesi's plates were 'the largest he has ever attempted in regular Architecture'.

Figure 93 'Details of the
Orders of Ante-room'

engraver was Pastorini, and more dully, in that for the eating room at Bowood
by Vivarez. While it is true that none of these plates equals the drama with
which Piranesi endowed his creations, they were several steps ahead of the
presentation of architectural details by Chambers or, for that matter, Stuart, both
of whom had a conventional, academic view of the architectural plate, little
changed from the seventeenth century. Equally progressive was the mixture of
furniture amongst the more decorative architectural details and this helped to

Figure 94 'Designs of different pieces of furniture'

give the plates the diversity and variety that both Adam and Piranesi sought in their graphic work. So much so, that Adam specifically mentioned in the description of the engravings, that furniture was 'here introduced, in order to give more utility and diversity to the work'.[44] Though furniture designs had appeared regularly in eighteenth-century pattern books such as those of Halfpenny and Kent or more spectacularly in Chambers' *Designs of Chinese buildings, furniture . . . utensils*, the actual mixture of furniture and architecture was rare. Adam in *The Works* included straightforward plates of his furniture, like the harpsichord for Catherine II of Russia, and the less straightforward combination of a hall table and chimney piece from Lansdowne House. The volume II engraving by Pastorini after an Adam drawing of 1774, showed a picturesque assembly of doors, curtain cornice, girandoles and a richly inlaid commode, all from Derby House, and assembled in the style of the Adam sketch for Kenwood (figure 88). A similar mixture was offered in plate VIII of the Luton Park group of 1775, again, and perhaps significantly, engraved by Pastorini (figure 94). It was possibly Pastorini and Piranesi who produced the most outstanding prints in *The Works* and the former's interior view of the drawing room at Derby House showed an unparalleled manipulation of space and light in an architectural engraving (figure 95).

The perspective views distributed throughout the various parts of *The Works*,

---

[44] *The Works*, I, part II, p. 10.

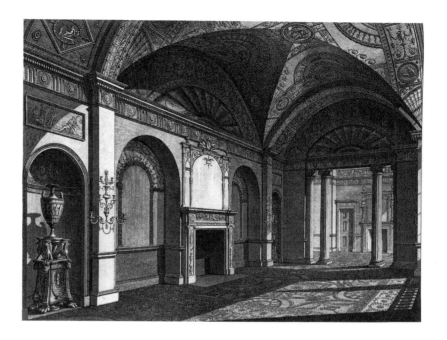

were not, in themselves, unusual in an architectural book at this time. The
ground had been broken not only by *The Ruins*, but by similar architectural
travel books, as well as by the plates from the *Antiquities of Athens*. But unlike all
of them, Adam showed contemporary rather than antique buildings and in this
way indirectly conferred on his work a sort of classical validity. Where the
antique did appear, as in the sculpture of the Syon plates, Adam cunningly
outlined the figures of the Laocoon and Dying Gaul against their contemporary setting with great clarity, especially in what was essentially an elevational
drawing (figure 96). These plates, dated 1761, perhaps marked the start of
Adam's exploration of the use of perspective within the conventions of the
architectural print. The end of such an experiment is seen in the interior of
Drury Lane of 1775 or better in the two perspectives of the Derby *fête-champêtre*,
of 1774, though they appeared in the posthumous third volume of *The Works*,
in 1822. With so many hands at work on the book, there was little stylistic
development apparent amongst the several engravers and a minimum level of
uniformity was enforced by the tight control Adam kept over his draughtsmen.

Of the nine perspective plates in the original two volumes of *The Works*, two
– Derby House and Drury Lane Theatre – were interior views. To these can be
added the *fête-champêtre* plates and the perspective of the interior of the gallery
at Syon, all of which appeared in the posthumous volume III. They did not
however, present a distinct group and though three of them were probably
engraved by Pastorini, the Derby *fête* pair were not. In drawing terms, the

Section of one End of the Hall, next to the great Apartment.   Coupe du Vestibule au Côté des grands Apartements.

Scale of   Feet.

Figure 96   'Sections of two
Ends of the Hall'

Section of one End of the Hall, next to the private Apartment. Coupe du Vestibule au Côté des Apartements particuliers.

Figure 97 'Inside view of
the Supper-room & part of
the Ball-room'

horseshoe-shaped supper and ballroom of Lord Derby's 'The Oaks' was
exploited to give both dramatic and closed perspectives, which was not the case
in the wide auditorium view from the Drury Lane stage, even though drama
was offered by the gesticulating figures on the second tier of the theatre loosely
derived from Piranesi's prints (figure 97). Robert Adam's keenness for such
figures went back to his Roman sketching days with Clérisseau and Piranesi and,
when at work in 1758 on *The Ruins*, he had suggested a collaboration between
Paul Sandby and the engraver Rooker to give human scale ('Rusticks') and
variety to the finished plates.[45] The figures in the *fête-champêtre* scenes were
much more lively and naturalistic than those drawn in many of the prints.
Certainly the receding supper table with its rioting diners contrasted as much
with the usual decorum of Adam's figures and peaceful abstract settings like the
Syon gallery or the Derby House dining room. The last two were outstanding
for the technique Adam and Pastorini devised to manipulate the verticals and
horizontals of the print to give the illusion of light, shadow and depth from a
range of sophisticated tonalities. It was the suggested light from the gallery and
drawing-room windows that held the Derby House engraving together, broke
the monotony of the perspective and so disguised the emptiness of the room
(figure 95). In the drawing room, too, the emphasis of the light reflected on the

[45] Fleming, 'Adam Miscellany', *Architectural Review*, p. 105.

126

Figure 98   'Design of a Bridge in imitation of the Aqueducts of the Ancients to be built over the lake at Bowood'

seemingly mirrored surfaces drew attention to Adam's description of the room in which the pilasters were covered in satin, and the door 'ornaments are painted on papier-maché, and so highly japanned as to appear like glass'.[46]

It was easier for Adam to suggest a picturesque character in the prints which had some landscape content and so allowed him to exploit atmosphere and hint at a mood. Dusk, gathering shadows, an overcast sky, were all subtly evoked in his plates for the ruined bridges at Syon and Bowood, and more ambitiously in his set piece for the illumination of the royal gardens of the Queen's House. While they lacked colour, or in Adam's version of the gouache, tinting, the Bowood print revealed best what a skilful engraver like Pastorini could achieve under Adam's direction. His sensitive hatching was able to suggest a low glancing light that caught the irregularities of the bridge's masonry and threw the whole foreground into the deepest shade that was eminently picturesque (figure 98). Cunego in his print for the Queen's House illumination explored similar territory with much the same Adam-inspired technique. Both rose to the royal commission – a birthday surprise by Queen Charlotte for George III – and the print was probably made after Robert Adam's drawings in Rome, under his brother's direction in 1762 (figures 99 and 100).[47] If such was the case, then

[46]   *The Works* II, part I, p. unnumbered.
[47]   *Ibid.*, I, part V, pl. V. The print, like those of Piranesi for *The Works*, was signed 'D. Cunego Sculp. Romae'. Cunego was part of James Adam's Roman establishment in 1761–2, see Fleming, *Robert Adam*, p. 371.

Figure 99 'Original Design
of an Illumination &
Transparency'

Clérisseau and the artificers of *The Ruins* could have had a hand in its
manufacture. In fact, the illumination and transparency put together as a
pavilion and colonnades suggested the elaborate tradition of the Roman
macchina del fuochi with which the Adam brothers and Clérisseau were
reasonably familiar, particularly the Roman *fuochi Farnesiani*.[48] But, in both
the drawing and plate, the formality of the architecture was overlaid with the
garden scenery and the engraver made the most of highlights and shadows to
suggest a *fête-champêtre* where the King was having the scene explained to him.
In all of this, Adam was trying to match the spirit of the print to landscape
themes that had been taken up in the earlier prefaces. For instance, the garden
at Kenwood had been praised as 'beautiful and picturesque', and a glimpse given
in the garden perspective of the house. At Luton, the unillustrated park was
described in picturesque language as 'diversified by gentle rising and fallings',
which created a 'variety in the views, and produce a striking effect in
landscape'.[49]

Adam's finished drawings for the royal illuminations and his pen sketch for
the layout of the Kenwood plate showed his actual involvement in print
making. This had been apparent in his correspondence with James Adam over

[48] Adam had seen the fireworks and illuminations at St Peter's and the Palazzo Farnese, Fleming,
Robert Adam, p. 177, and included in the 1818 sale was 'Fuochi d'Artifizio da Specchi Parocel'.
(Bolton, *Architecture*, II, p. 330.)

[49] *The Works*, I, part III, p. unnumbered.

Figure 100   Robert Adam,
*Drawing for the Illumination and
Transparency, for Plate V of The
Works*

illustrations for *The Ruins*, where he had shown himself as a hard master, constantly critical. He never abandoned his technical interest and as late as 1782, with both *The Ruins* and *Works* well behind him, he was still experimenting and revising. He wrote then to his brother-in-law and amateur etcher, John Clerk of Eldin, advising about the sort of illustrations needed in a book on naval tactics that Clerk had in mind. Adam recommended the fashionable acquaforte process which he promised, 'I will write it down step by step as we proceed & will by the end of the week be able to give you some account of it. I would like in your plates for the Tactics that you would draw pretty little tiny ships, and the Starboard and Larboard tacks, or dashing down on the Enemy. The aquatints would do charming for the bonny wee sailings. You would do them as fast as you could cast peas in your mouth' (figure 101).[50] Adam was as good as his word, and Clerk acknowledged receipt of the aquatint process shortly afterwards. Adam's source for all of this was probably the versatile Paul Sandby, who had greatly popularised the process in the 1770s, and probably included Adam among his converts. Certainly, it would have come close to the effect he sought in his tinted watercolours and had striven after in the engraved perspectives of *The Works*. A hint of such a move away from the limitations of the tonal engraving and the unsatisfactory nature of colouring up the prints by hand was clearly signalled in *The Works*. Adam wrote there that 'We have

[50] A. A. Tait, 'Robert Adam and John Clerk of Eldin', *Master Drawings* 4 (1978) p. 54.

Figure 101   John Clerk, *An Essay on Naval Tactics* (1804)

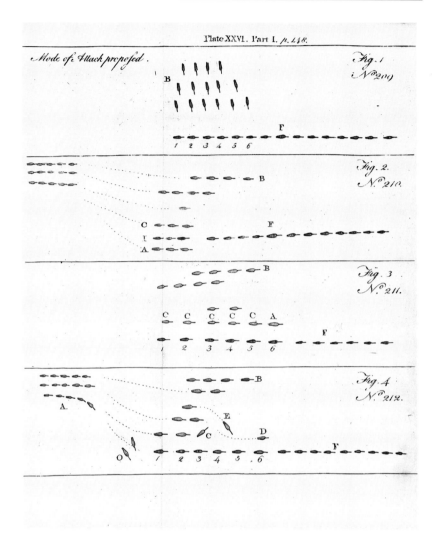

thought it proper to colour with the tints, used in the execution, a few copies of each number', but it was not a proposal that he pursued with enthusiasm or conviction.[51] To any artist with strong picturesque leanings, the game of hand colouring or tinting on any scale must have been over with the appearance, in 1775 of Sandby's series of Welsh views in aquatint.

Robert Adam's attitude to print making never stood still, either in the image

[51] *The Works*, I, part I, p. 7; this was repeated with less enthusiasm in part II, p. 7 as, 'we have published a few copies of this number with the ceiling coloured, as it is executed in the work it self, and have, on that account, been obliged to fix the price of those copies at twenty four shillings'. This was the library ceiling in tints of pink and green which reduced 'the glare' of white.

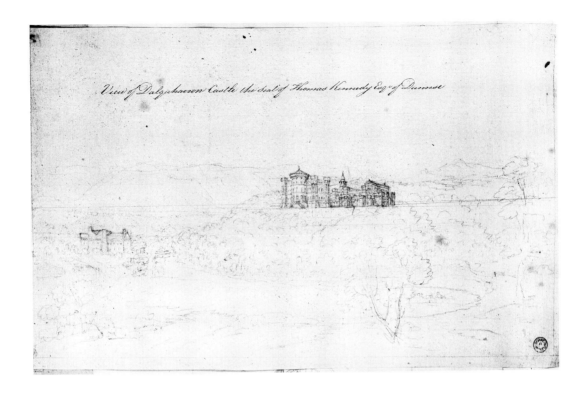

caught or in the technique used for its realisation. For such a mind, the plates as
well as the text of *The Works* suggested ways in which the picturesque might be
explored. The chosen form was the landscape panorama, executed in pencil or
pen and probably intended for engraving at the outset. Its origins lay in the
landscape prints of Marco Ricci and the garden landscapes Adam had invented
in Rome with Lallemand, where a balance had been struck between building
and setting. The melting pot for such disparate images was the picturesque and
the mixing spoon was the tentative theorising of *The Works*. The incomplete
pencil view that Adam made of Dalquharran in Ayrshire, with its old and new
Adam castle set round a lake, was typical of the sympathy sought between
building and siting, and the resonance of past to present (figure 102). The more
finished pen drawing of a circular building in a heavily wooded panorama
repeated more engagingly the same, essential balance between the two elements
(figure 103). The foreground clumps and rough grasses were a foil to the large
office court, designed in the style of a roman camp, peacefully and modestly
set on a rise in the middle distance.[52] So successful was the landscape scene that
its purpose to show the proposed offices for Brampton Bryan was almost lost

Figure 102   Robert Adam,
'View of Dalquharran Castle'

[52] Soane Museum, AV XXXVII, ff. 59–61.

Figure 103   Robert Adam, *Panorama of a castellated building in woodland setting*

Figure 104   Robert Adam, *Unfinished drawing for a Castle invention*

sight of. Its feeling was not greatly different to a similarly unfinished sketch for one of Adam's castle inventions (figure 104). The appearance of these drawings as prints can be glimpsed in the rather conventional engraving published in Angus' *Views of Seats*, of Oxenfoord Castle taken from an Adam drawing.[53] It can hardly have matched his expectations, and fell far short of the surviving

[53] For Adam at Oxenfoord see, A. A. Tait, *The Landscape Garden in Scotland* (Edinburgh, 1980), pp. 110–13.

Figure 105 Robert Adam,
'Oxenfoord in Scotland, the
Seat of Sir John Dalrymple'

Figure 106 Robert Adam,
*Watercolour of Oxenfoord Castle
from the park*

watercolours of the park and castle which better explored the ideal fusion of castle and scenery (figures 105 and 106). A rather more picturesque alternative appeared in a proof engraving of a Ruisdael style tree, signed with a reversed 'RA' (figure 107). This print – which may be his – grasped better than the Angus view the richness and roughness that Adam had developed in his landscapes since the appearance of the garden engravings of *The Works*.

Figure 107   Robert Adam (?),
Two trees in leaf, engraving

Of the two Adam books published during their lifetime, *The Works* was
undoubtedly the more important. It marked as dramatic a watershed in the
brothers' careers as *The Ruins* had done in laying to rest juvenile plans and
ambitions. If *The Ruins* looked backwards to a collective experience gained,
then *The Works* explored a more complicated closing and opening of doors.
This was boldly set out in many of the plates whose content, composition and
technique, all combined to distinguish new horizons. The inclusion of
furniture, the emphasis on the decorative arts, the sophisticated visual overlapping of one plate with another and the visual symmetry of the engravings, all
made *The Works* a *tour de force* of a high order. The book expanded through its
plates the comprehension of architecture and so extended the boundaries of
what was accepted as part of architecture. The brothers, in this way, finally
broke with a classicism of precise and restrictive categories already fractured by
The Ruins. The resulting vacuum was to be filled by the rethought and renewed
Adam styles, best represented by the flexibility of the picturesque. The very
ambiguity of the disparate prefaces mirrored the fragmentary aspect of such a
liberal, architectural philosophy whose emphasis on experiment and variety
could be succinctly, perhaps crudely, expressed as the end justifying the means.

5

The picturesque style

MOST ARCHITECTS' DRAWINGS are a means to an end which is the building. Adam was different. Any drawing – even the slightest of sketches – was part of an intricate creative process, revealing at a variety of levels and to be kept at all cost. Such an attitude was to be expected from a collector and connoisseur of drawings and it was understandable if he saw much of his own work from such a standpoint. The first sketch was the *disegno*, and for him, the heart of any scheme which made the wash, watercolour, or thumbnail sketch as indispensable as the survey plan. The brothers' energies were concentrated in this first breath of creation, and the more mechanical processes of design – essentially the working up of the drawings – were devolved to their draughtsmen, trained as surrogate Adams. Such an emphasis on the sketch in the chain of command perhaps explained why so many have survived and why often the most casual were signed and dated.

The method Robert Adam used to turn the most informal of sketches into a recognisable architectural project was again very much his own. His three-dimensional thinking appreciated the essential, painterly qualities of the perspective and how effective watercolour and wash could be in setting the spirit and mood for such a scheme. It was a fertile field for a talented water-colourist like Adam, passionately committed to the picturesque landscape. Yet, as has been said, Adam was idiosyncratic rather than innovatory. He was largely following in the footsteps of William Kent, who shared a painterly approach to architecture and the perspective drawing. Kent had recognised as well, the complementary roots of architecture and landscape, and the emerging part to be played by the landscape gardener in both worlds (figure 112).[1] In all of this, Adam was responding to the growing movement of the picturesque and certainly such sensitivity to the new style was apparent in the various prefaces to

---

[1] For Kent's landscape drawings see, John Dixon Hunt, *William Kent, Landscape Garden Designer* (London, 1987), pp. 41–9.

The Works. It was hardly a coincidence that his picturesque drawings were revived around 1774, when *The Works* started to appear in print. Though the drawing form revived, was based on the evocative *capricci* of Clérisseau and Lallemand, it was given in its second coming a new and distinctly northern twist.

Though 1774 may be taken as a turning point, the picturesque composition had a long history in Robert Adam's work. It can be traced back to the copies he made after the landscape prints of Marco Ricci in the early 1750s and to a strong dose of Sandby's Scottish drawings he received around the same time. Onto such a youthful taste was grafted the picturesque classicism of the Roman topographers, and the fruits of such a style were evident in Adam's landscape proposals for Kedleston. The two pen and watercolour sketches he suggested for the park seemed rather like a landscape by Kent, drawn by Lallemand, and only hinted at the picturesque vision of the 1770s, with its exploitation of muted tones and irregularity (figure 108, plate 6). Such tones were the means by which Adam set the mood of his drawings and this was complemented by coarse and irregular details which subtly emphasised the asymmetry of composition. There was little of this in the early sixties, although both the brothers had arrived in and left Italy with their picturesque prejudices reinforced. In 1756, fresh to Italy, Robert Adam extolled the new landscape in essentially picturesque terms where architecture was boldly accepted as scenery. It was, he wrote, 'the most intoxicating Country in the world, for a pictoresque Hero, would you have agreeable smiling prospects, they are here in abundance. Would you dip into wild caverns, where glimmering light aggravate the horrid view of Rocks & Cavitys & pools of water. Here there are many of them, such indeed as my wildest imagination had never pictured to me.'[2] A rather less enthusiastic and more calculating response was James Adam's careful theorising of 1762, where he thoughtfully explored the relationship between landscape and architecture. He dealt with light and shade, the use of contours and so on, much as though he was describing one of his brother's picturesque watercolours of the 1780s, however, he studiously avoided using the term picturesque.[3] Over a decade later, his opinions had changed remarkably little, and when he wrote his preface for *The Works* in 1774, he still treated the picturesque as a common ground between landscape painting and architecture and essentially a theoretical concept.[4] It may be that unlike his brother, James Adam never succumbed to the full charms of the movement and remained sceptical. Certainly, his response to the picturesque after 1774 was rational if not functional and clearly spelt out in his *Practical Essays on Agriculture* of 1789, where

[2] SRO GD 18/4803.   [3] Fleming, *Robert Adam*, pp. 315–16.   [4] See p. 112.

136

Figure 108   Robert Adam,
*Sketch for landscaping the park at
Kedelston*

the ideal landscape admired was the cultivated and improved one, praised for good husbandry and better economics.

In the Adam sale catalogues of both 1818 and 1821, several lots were described as framed and glazed watercolours by Robert Adam. They were further recommended by the auctioneer in the rather flowery language of their kind as 'highly finished' and 'original inventions'.[5] In this, he was making no distinction between them and the other watercolours being sold at this time from the rest of the collections. To his professional eye, Adam's drawings had set out to please and stimulate the imagination and that was a hard enough task without enquiring after any further or deeper meaning. That such drawings might have a more complicated history was Robert Adam's doing and that they might have a more practical role was his choice as well. For Adam, there was only a short step, perhaps downhill, from these framed inventions to the larger panels of a similar ruined antiquity that he stylishly drew in his sections for Headford and Home Houses to be worked up by Zucchi.[6] His surviving sketches make quite clear that they were part of Adam's original decorative programme where antiquity ruined and restored (by Adam) was dramatically and physically contrasted (figures 109 and 110). A smaller, but rather more distinct group, was formed by the early Adam drawings for architecture with a landscape background. His drawing for the Doric gate at Kedleston, of 1759, was typical of this sort of composition where a landscape setting has been added

5   Bolton, *Architecture*, II, p. 331.
6   For such an interpretation see Paul Oppé, 'Robert Adam's Picturesque Compositions', *Burlington Magazine* 80 (1942), pp. 56–9. The Headford drawings are shown in John Harris, *Headford House & Robert Adam* (London, 1973); for Home House see, AV XIV, ff. 119, 132, 134, and Margaret Whinney, *Home House* (London, 1969), p. 74. For the iconography of the Home panels see *Ibid.*, p. 38.

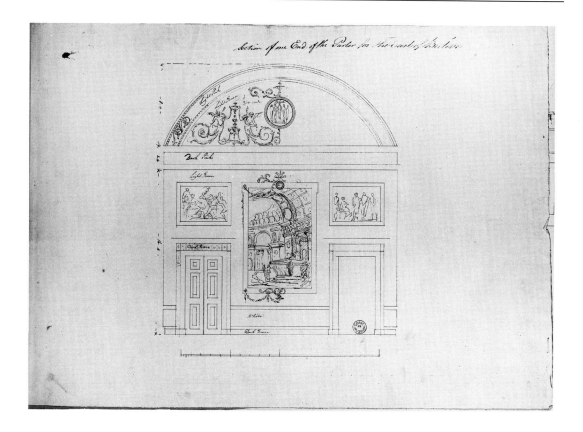

Figure 109 Adam Office,
Headford, 'Section of one
End of the Parlor'

to a straightforward architectural drawing to make it more appealing (figure 111). There is not a great deal to choose between this and Chambers' similar watercolour for Sherborne Castle of around the same time.[7] Both architects looked back to their Roman academy days and Clérisseau's instruction in the sentimental view and caught the style but not the spirit of their sophisticated instructor. Perhaps in more parochial terms, Robert Adam capitalised on William Kent's drawings in which architecture and landscape were mixed in a suggestive way that made him outstanding amongst his rococo contemporaries. It was a small, Kent wash drawing of this kind for a woodland hermitage that Adam owned, presumably for that reason (figure 112). It was better but not greatly different from the pretty designs for grottoes and arbours in a supremely artificial setting, shown in a book like Thomas Wright's *Universal Architecture*.[8] Such whimsical projects represented an unthinking tradition from which Kent and later Adam distanced themselves.

[7] The Kedleston gateway is illustrated in Harris, *Robert Adam and Kedleston*, p. 76; for Sherborne see Harris, *Sir William Chambers*, pl. 79, p. 24.

[8] Thomas Wright, *Universal Architecture*, ed. Eileen Harris (London, 1979).

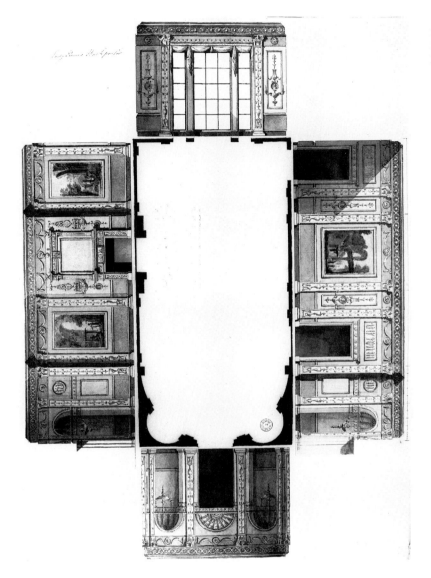

Figure 110 Adam Office, Home House, 'Lady Homes Back parlor'

The most obvious link in Adam's work with the rococo past, was in his garden architecture and especially in its cynosure, the cottage orné. His cottage drawings possibly highlighted best such a rococo blurring of design and decoration which were allowed, for once to overlay Adam functionalism. In fact, the cottage whether orné or not, summed up for the eighteenth century a response which was inseparable from that of the picturesque. It was an evocative symbol, redolent of social attitudes and historical associations that stretched to include a range of rustic and farm buildings. In its fundamental form as the primitive hut, it symbolised the simple life of Rousseau as well as the

Figure 111 Robert Adam,
Kedleston, *Design for the north
lodge*

Figure 112 William Kent,
*Arcadian hermitage in a
woodland*

evolutionary theories of Laugier and Chambers.[9] It had been illustrated as the
basic architectural dwelling in the latter's *Civil Architecture*, of 1759, repeated in
more fanciful form as the frontispiece to Laugier's *Essai sur l'architecture* of 1755,
and in Piranesi's *Della Magnificenza*. Something of this architectural descent as

[9] For Laugier's concept of the hut see, Herrmann, *Laugier*, pp. 43–52; and for Chambers', Harris,
Sir William Chambers, pp. 134–5.

Figure 113   Robert Adam,
*Primitive seat for Mrs Kennedy
at Dalquharran*

well as a close reading of Laugier was clearly set out in Adam's watercolour of
around 1785 for an arbour seat at Dalquharran where raw and rooted tree trunks
support the roof, as much as primitive columns as vaults, with the same
construction repeated in a more developed way in the background cottage
(figure 113, plate 5). These tree trunks appeared again in his watercolour
for a thatched lodge of 1787, where their theoretical significance was matched
by the wooden construction of the roof and its embryonic classical detail
(figure 114).

   Much the same sort of cottage appeared frequently in Adam's work, when he
had some cottage-style house in mind. The rather coarse watercolour in the
National Gallery of Scotland showed a lumpy, primitive and rather ugly cottage,
asymmetrical in composition, and sited at the bottom of a cliff beside a river
(figure 115). It was just the sort of image – rustic, informal, nostalgic – that
appealed to the picturesque eye both then and now. It appeared throughout the
movement from Gainsborough's landscape drawings, to the wash sketches used
by William Gilpin to illustrate his popular tours (figure 125). Indeed, it is easy
to find Adam influenced by both these artists. His couple of drawings of figures
at a cave in the Blair Adam collection skilfully repeat Gilpin's handling of a
similar subject (figure 116), and a group of rough charcoal sketches on coloured
paper were just as close to the spirit and technique of Gainsborough's chalk
landscapes of the 1780s. The *Landscape with Castle* of 1787/8 or his *Figures and
Horses on a Country Road* of about the same time both come near Adam's
compositions, especially to the architectonic character of the buildings (figure

Figure 114   Robert Adam,
Elevation for a primitive cottage

Figure 115   Robert Adam,
Cottage at the bottom of a cliff

Figure 116   Robert Adam,
Figures in a Cave

117).[10] Gainsborough's cottage and lodge buildings on either side of his
country road seem little different in their irregularity, roughness and haphazard
composition from several similar, fluid designs in the Soane Museum (figure
118). There was little to choose between the artist's and the architect's approach
to the picturesque building except that Adam had, at some undetermined stage,
a commission in mind.

There was no key date for Adam's cottage designs, nor, any significant
shift in their composition. The large or small cottage had always been a form
inseparable from the landscape movement in any of its phases, and was perhaps
both over-familiar and undervalued, that is until the arrival of the cult of the
primitive in the 1750s. Perhaps, Adam shared Gilpin's prejudice, that the finest
scene calls for 'every appendage of grandeur to harmonize with it. The cottage
offends. It should be a castle, a bridge, an aqueduct, or some object that suits its
dignity.'[11] Like the castles, they appeared in early Adam *capricci* and surfaced in
his Roman drawings of around 1756, cast as the tiled and shuttered forms of the
casa colonica of the *campagna*. In the seventies and eighties, these cottages took on
a more national air with tile replaced by thatch, walls constructed out of a
variety of materials, and, like the castle inventions, composed as tumbledown,

[10] John Hayes, *The Drawings of Thomas Gainsborough* 2 vols., (London, 1970); apart from the
cottage door style of architecture, Gainsborough showed in the 1780s considerable architectural
interest, see *ibid.*, I, p. 229, and II, pls. 166, 167. For Robert Adam's appreciation of his drawings
see p. 71.
[11] William Gilpin, *Remarks on Forest Scenery* 2 vols., (London, 1808), I, p. 227.

Figure 117 Thomas
Gainsborough, *Cottages and
figures on a road*

asymmetrical buildings rooted to their setting (figure 115). In few of these
respects were they, in any way, different from the genre and only a group
amongst the Adam volumes were outstanding in their Gainsborough-like
roughness or use of coloured paper.[12] However, unlike the canvas cottages of
Gainsborough, Moreland, or Wheatley, they lacked any social voice and instead
appeared to emphasise in a nostalgic way an architectural sense of the past, a
mood that was true of Adam's castle landscapes as well. Few of these rustic
hovels or superior estate cottages can be pinned to any special period, or any
specific message read into them. There were no references to the seasons nor to
the labour of the countryside, nor were there any obvious scenes of hay
making, harvesting, hunting, or even peasant gambols. The husbandry these
drawings did reveal was as rudimentary as the elemental landscape setting – the
cloddish figures tend and move oxen and goats between patches of pasture in
a poor, often mountainous landscape where nature dominates man. In this
fashion, Adam followed Gilpin who was prepared to tolerate the cottage in a
mixed landscape on condition that 'the appendages of husbandry, and every idea
of cultivation, we wish them to totally disappear'.[13] Such a primeval landscape
was the reverse of the new model countryside of the agricultural revolution,

[12] Soane Museum, AV II, ff. 78–82, AV IV, ff. 1–26.
[13] Gilpin, *Forest Scenery*, I, p. 112.

realised in the country-house paintings of Stubbs and Richard Wilson, and analysed and praised in James Adam's own *Practical Essays on Agriculture*, of 1789.

Figure 118   Robert Adam, *Thatched cottage and sketch plan*

The cottages themselves, presented much the same sort of contrast with eighteenth-century notions of propriety and convenience. They were rarely the homes of the industrious poor, where Gilpin's ideal that 'happiness may reside, unsupported by wealth', was to be found. Like the picturesque castles, they were frequently decayed and often salvaged from the ruins of the larger, grander buildings beside which they squatted. Their age was hidden by the various materials of their construction and they recalled not so much a picturesque character as an overwhelming sense of history. They were without doubt the exact opposite of the utilitarian cottage described by James Adam in volume II of the *Essays on Agriculture* where painted, cast iron was recommended as an appropriate and economical building material.[14] Instead Robert Adam pursued nostalgia. His Copenhagen drawing of a tiny hamlet crouching beside some great Roman bridge of antiquity comprised three cottages hewn from stone and plaster with roofs thatched or constructed out of old planks of wood (figure 119). In the middle distance was a two-storeyed, irregular farmhouse

[14] Tait, *Landscape Garden*, p. 104; and see more generally John Martin Robinson, *Georgian Model Farms* (Oxford, 1983), pp. 107–12.

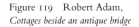

Figure 119   Robert Adam,
Cottages beside an antique bridge

with a tiled roof which made the cottages seem even more miserable and primitive. The contrast between the bridge and the cottages, that is to say between public and vernacular architecture, could hardly be more strongly contrived and had already appeared in the rustic bridge for Syon, shown in volume II of *The Works*. Such an interpretation – stretched a little further – suggested that Adam offered in these almost genre scenes his version of the human predicament where decline was symbolised by the hand-to-mouth existence at the cottage-watermill, the restricted self-sufficiency of the fisherman and the dejected cattle. They all represented in their way, a rural squalor which evoked a vivid contrast with the past bustle and energy of the organised commercial life that had passed along the imperial bridge. It was a subtle and graphic reminder of the message from the introduction to *The Ruins* that a past will inevitably be judged by its public monuments.

There were probably few distinct steps between these evocative cottage landscapes and the cottage orné designed in the Adam office. As simple buildings with limited and rudimentary planning, the shift from sketchbook to the office drawing board was an easy one, especially for a temperament like Robert Adam's. The seemingly frivolous design for a form of Laugier's primitive hut, masked as a garden arbour for Adam's niece Mrs Kennedy at Dalquharran, was typical of such a visual approach (figure 113). More light-hearted than frivolous, was a pen and ink drawing of 1786 for a small lodge on the London Road. It showed a one room building with a minute campanile

146

Figure 120   Robert Adam,
'Lodge near the Lane being
the approach to the House
from London'

and bell, tall chimney stack, and on the woodland track an extraordinary Dick
Whittington group with a dog walking on its hindlegs, pursued by a cat (figure
120). Together they formed a composition as much bizarre as picturesque. The
extreme example of such seeming spontaneity and casualness was perhaps
Adam's use of a torn-off page from his appointments diary as paper for his first
thoughts on the design for a cottage group.[15] Whether this rather than the
drawing board was the invariable Adam method of composition can only be
guessed at but it ensured that invention dominated and was respected. But
possibly the most fundamental difference between these picturesque cottage
drawings and Adam's actual projects was his attitude towards symmetry. It was
only in his later cottage commissions that he came near to matching the
irregularity of his inventions, and the extreme, higgledy-piggledy estate
cottages at the entrance to a wooded park of his Huntington wash drawing was

---

[15] Soane Museum, AV II, f. 171.

Figure 121   Robert Adam,
View of a castellated gate-lodge

never repeated quite so boldly in his architectural work (figure 121). And in this lay the answer to the time and energy Adam spent on these overlapping and endlessly varied picturesque drawings. Their role was to stimulate and inspire, and so provide an immediate imaginative quarry, with inventions more daring than practical, and ones that emphasised setting and mood. Rather like Reynolds, Adam perhaps felt that a building should rely on its actual setting for much of its essential variety and irregularity.[16]

The companion to the cottage was the castle and both reflected an artistic vocabulary derived from contemporary literature. As such, they were the visual equivalents of the paper castles of Otranto or Vathek, or the idealised cottages of Charlotte Smith. But in Adam's hands such buildings were a far cry from a generalised statement about this aspect of the picturesque and, apart from the small, repetitive washes and watercolours of towers or keeps, they shared a quite specific architectural form. Invariably, all were in decay and showed crumbling walls and ruined battlements, though, at first glance this was not always apparent. They differed, in this way, from the traditional castle of the picturesque artist where the passage of time was measured by the degree of ruination (figure 122). They also had a fairly obvious plan. The most common was the straightforward motte and bailey arrangement which had been

[16] Joshua Reynolds, *Discourses*, ed. Roger Fry (London, 1905), pp. 367–8.

148

Figure 122   Robert Adam, *Castle beside a river*

overlaid with an irregular development of curtain walls incorporating an extraordinary variety of towers – square, round, semicircular, partial octagon. The castles themselves lacked much decorative detail, apart that is from their obvious military statement through battlements and machicolations. Their inspiration was very much the workaday Norman castle rather than the sophisticated works of the fifteenth century. Nothing showed this better than the windows which were the basic arrow slits or crosslets with only the occasional refinement of a single or double lancet window. For all Adam's considerable topographic and antiquarian knowledge, such castles rarely had a particular source. Instead, they covered the gamut of his practice, from a military complex like Alnwick in Northumberland, which he had restored in the 1760s, to the simpler Scottish tower houses such as Culzean or Barnbougle.[17] Their setting, however, was always logical enough, and buildings, as often as not, commanded some strategic pass or ford, or dominated a valley from a defensible outcrop of rock (figure 123). They did not, in landscape terms, differ greatly from the crenellated concoctions of Sandby, Gilpin or Cozens except in the greater emphasis they placed on the castle as a structure. Just as familiar were Adam's

---

[17] For such commissions see Colvin, *Dictionary*, pp. 52–5. A good example of Robert Adam's use of the tower rather than castle in his watercolours was reproduced in Tait, *Robert Adam at Home*, p. 22, no. 58.

Figure 123 Robert Adam,
Castle on a rock beside a river

figures of the bandit type, borrowed from Salvator Rosa or similar landscape printmakers of the seventeenth century, where small figures of a vaguely military type escorted a wagon of plunder back to the robber baron's lair (figure 124, plate 4). Small and indistinct, often in shadow, their role was a minor one, as much to suggest movement as to make an effective foil to the large building they so laboriously approached. They rarely distracted the eye from the castle.

In some ways, these drawings should be considered as a sort of architectural stream-of-consciousness where the most simple concepts of architectural composition were casually explored much in the same fashion as Alexander Cozens had used blots to direct his picturesque endeavours and fire his imagination. Such concentrated freedom made these castle drawings a powerful force in Adam's imagination, certainly more so than Sandby's tame topographic accuracy or Gilpin's blander and generalised castle scenery in Wales (figure 125). While Adam's castles were always picturesque, they were at the same time exceptionally gloomy and cheerless places. They penetrated the introspective and depressive side of Romanticism to the extent that they tyrannised both figures and landscape. The country itself was constructed from the most elemental, if not brutal, forms of mountains, rivers, rocks, all of which harmonised with the oppressive fortress-castle itself (figure 124). They had conspicuously little in common with Adam's light-hearted gothic projects of the

Figure 124   Robert Adam,
*Castle on a rock approached by
figures*

Figure 125   William Gilpin,
'First view of Dinevawr-
castle'

1750s and 1760s.[18] If these drawings are taken as capturing the mood of their creator, then it was a defensive and wary one, well hidden behind Adam's ebullient public face. The castle, as Adam pictured it, symbolised an enduring form which had withstood all vicissitudes to remain battered but unbowed. In this fashion, it was not unlike the architect himself.

[18] Fleming, *Robert Adam*, pp. 81–3.

Figure 126 Robert Adam,
*Sketch design for Barnbougle
Castle*

The outstanding transition from drawing to commission was the Barnbougle
scheme of 1774. It ushered in the renewed picturesque phase in Robert Adam's
work for which the brothers had trailed their coats in *The Works*. Adam was
asked by the third Earl of Rosebery to make designs for converting the L-shaped
sixteenth-century castle of Barnbougle, strategically placed on the edge of the
Firth of Forth, into a new house in 1774.[19] Both Adam and Rosebery appeared
to have settled on preservation and expansion in the castle style at the very
outset. This was borne out by two preliminary sketch drawings, one pen, the
other watercolour, each of much the same size (figure 126, plate 7). Both
showed the entrance facade of the proposed castle and it is impossible to say
which was the earlier. Whatever slight differences there were between the two,
seem to be those of drawing technique rather than design. The next stage was
shown by a group of pencil and ink, office drawings in the Soane Museum.
These Soane drawings showed the translation of the two sketched into more
formal architectural drawings, made to scale on the drawing board (figure 127).
While they lacked much of the sparkle of the first two design sketches, they
showed a reasonably smooth transition from project to plan. Yet, even in these
somewhat prosaic drawings, the building was not finally fixed, and redrawings,
over-drawings, reworkings and inking-in, all showed the creative process
continuing while Adam stepped back as the drawings became more mechanical
and the draughtsman replaced the artist.[20] But, for all this graphic heart-
searching, the ultimate scheme for the castle had moved remarkably little from

[19] A. A. Tait, 'Robert Adam's Picturesque Architecture', *Burlington Magazine* 123 (1981) pp. 421–2.
[20] *Ibid.*, p. 421.

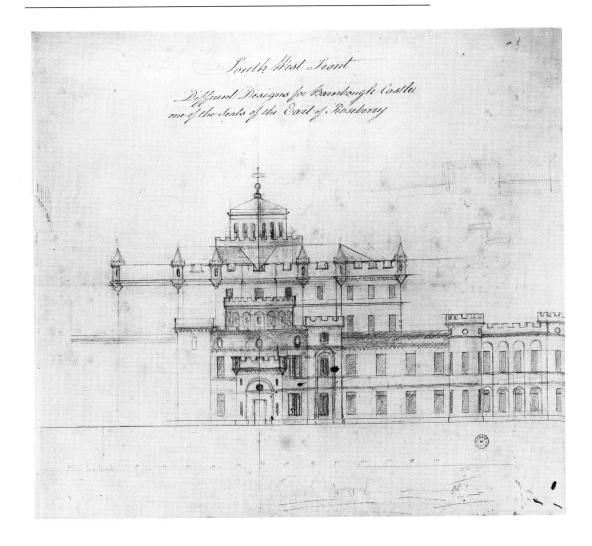

South West Front

*Different Designs for Barnbougle Castle
one of the seats of the Earl of Rosebery*

the first set of pencil drawings. The biggest jump had been between them and the evocative watercolour at the very start and heart of the commission.

Though the original notion of Barnbougle as a medieval keep with a double triangular plan was a constant one, the dramatic contrast between the motte and bailey has been lost in the transition. The height of the bailey was reduced in all the Soane drawings and the elaboration of detail on its battlements and pepper-pot turrets diminished its stark and aggressive form. Similarly, the excessive horizontal emphasis on the flanking wings turned the design from a vertical to a horizontal one. But the outstanding loss was the picturesque silhouette. The pitched roofs of the two flanking buildings have been removed and replaced by flat ones, hidden behind the battlements of the wall heads (figure 128). The seriousness of this loss was apparent, in the Adam perspective views of the

Figure 127 Adam Office, 'South West Front: Different Designs for Barnbougle Castle'

153

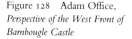

Figure 128   Adam Office,
*Perspective of the West Front of
Barnbougle Castle*

building of which all four (and two plans) were closely derived from the Soane elevations and plans. To make them more attractive and give them some sort of topical appeal, Adam provided a cloak of realism. Ships and a small harbour were suitable for the east front, a carriage and callers at the *porte-cochère* for the west (figure 38).[21] Both, and particularly the west perspective, showed a confusing sense of scale, where the figure beneath the tree in the foreground made the scale of those around the *porte-cochère* much too large. They gave, in turn, the castle a toy-like appearance, far different from the soaring, forbidding fortress of the watercolour sketch. Both the figures and vegetation of the west perspective were the handiwork of the figure draughtsman of the day, and lacked the subtlety and sense of place found in the picturesque drawings. This was no doubt inevitable when Robert Adam switched from explaining his building in pictorial terms to architectural ones. Detail and the conventions of draughts-manship – black windows, geometric shadows, even tones – have replaced the colour and free shapes of the first watercolour.

The Barnbougle drawings showed Adam's method of work in 1774. They were hardly likely to be exceptional and suggest that many of the picturesque drawings of the 1780s went through the same sort of evolutionary process. The distinction and considerable importance of the Barnbougle scheme was that its date put down a firm marker. The picturesque drawings and inventions after this

[21] *Ibid.*

Figure 129 Robert Adam,
*View of the office court for
Kirkdale*

date laid bare the roots of a new architectural style as well as the glimmerings of
fresh commissions, all of which went a long way to explain Adam's almost
obsessive indulgence in the picturesque drawing and watercolour. The con-
fusion between *capriccio* and sketch design was probably a deliberate one, typical
of the picturesque, and exploited in the pictorial arrangement of *The Works*.
Such ambiguity of purpose was apparent in the scattered drawings, all of around
1786, for a vast office court proposed for Kirkdale, in Kircudbrightshire (figure
129).[22] All have an independent artistic existence and it is only with hindsight
that their alternative purpose as part of Adam's compositional method becomes
apparent. As with Barnbougle, the inspiration of the entire design hung upon a
free and atmospheric wash drawing, reasonably accepted as an end in itself and
called appropriately enough *The Red Castle* (figure 130). In this dramatic sketch,
all the essential elements that Adam put together architecturally – circular stable
block, towered gateway, *enceinte* walls and various smaller towers – were
combined in an asymmetrical composition. It was, in fact, a reworking and
re-combination of earlier projects like the castle for Osterley or the decayed but
magnificent romanesque camp doubling as an office court for Brampton Bryan
in Hertfordshire, of the 1770s (figure 131).[23] Both *The Red Castle* and powerful
wash of Brampton Bryan gained much of their vigour probably by being Robert
Adam's first stab at a commission. The later panoramic view which showed
Brampton Bryan in the middle distance was less forceful and possibly intended

[22] *Ibid.*, p. 422.
[23] The Osterley Castle is illustrated in, *Victoria and Albert Museum: Robert Adam*, p. 54; and for
Brampton Bryan, see p. 131, and Soane Museum AV XXVII, f. 59.

Figure 130   Robert Adam,
The Red Castle

for tinting and washing in the style of Adam's contemporary view of Crossraguel
Abbey (figure 134), or turning into a landscape print like that for Oxenfoord
(figure 105).[24] Like the other panoramas or the Ayrshire castles of Dalquharran
and Culzean, there was some sort of graphic and commercial fate probably in
store for them all.[25]

The projects for Barnbougle and Kirkdale showed how Adam developed his
architectural schemes between 1774 and 1787 at least. They suggested that the
numerous picturesque inventions made so extensively in the 1780s had a direct
rather than parallel relationship with many of his buildings. While Adam's pure
landscape drawings were couched in the most familiar picturesque language and
offered only a general insight into his mind and taste, those of a more architectural bias did provide a starting point for actual projects. All served, however, as
an imaginative quarry to be mined at a variety of levels where some of the
material needed less fashioning than others. By this means, several of the watercolours or drawings could ultimately be pressed into architectural service more
easily than others. The cottages make that plain; the castles were more complex.
Some of Robert Adam's variations on the centralised castle theme, easily shaded
into a project such as that of 1777 for the unexecuted Beauly Castle, in Ross and
Cromarty (figure 132).[26] Others, such as a small, finely tinted drawing, almost a
miniature, for a grand castellated gateway captured a mood and time of day that
made it a remarkable generalised statement (figure 133, plate 8). That it can be

[24] See p. 132.   [25] Tait, *Landscape Garden*, pp. 110–13.
[26] Tait, 'Robert Adam's Picturesque Architecture', p. 422.

Figure 131 Robert Adam,
*Proposal for an office court for
Brampton Bryan*

Figure 132 Robert Adam,
Design for a centralised castle

linked to Adam's project for the entrance to Drummond Castle of around 1790 showed just how complex and difficult understanding the working of the quarry seams could be.[27]

An element essential to any picturesque drawing was mood. It was one that Adam exploited to the full in his use of both wash and watercolour, as might be expected from an architect who used colour as a critical part of all his architectural schemes. There was in this, a striking contrast between the high, rather harsh colours introduced by Manocchi to the office in the 1760s and the subdued gouache or tinting practised by Adam, himself, in many of these inventions. The distinction was clearly set out in a contemporary appreciation of his career where a distinction was made between 'his many architectural

[27] For an office copy drawing of the Drummond scheme see AV LI, f. 86, titled 'Plan and Elevation of a Castellated Gate & Lodge for Drummond Castle'.

Figure 133 Robert Adam,
*Sketch proposal for a castellated
Gate and lodge for Drummond
Castle*

drawings finished by his Clerk', and the 'infinite number of Valuable pieces, washed with water-colours, as well as what he has executed in Charo Obscuro, with Indian ink studied intirely for the General effect'.[28] His obituary in the *Gentleman's Magazine* specifically referred to them when it noted in 1792 that Adam's 'talents extended beyond the line of his own profession: he displayed in his numerous drawings in landscape a luxuriance of composition, and an effect of light and shadow, which have scarcely ever been equalled'.[29] Though allowing for an obvious degree of sympathetic exaggeration, it was clear that the ingenuity and variety of his castle and cottage inventions were held equal to his talents as a colourist or rather tinter.

The source for all such opinion was his incipient hagiographer John Clerk. He judged his brother-in-law generously, without hint of rivalry. Both men had been early pupils of Sandby in Scotland, and shared much the same antiquarian tastes, especially for castles. However, Adam had moved on – and well beyond Clerk's Sunday-artist temperament, which limited him as a talented topographer and engraver who later turned to Adam for advice. The form this took can be seen in the view they made, possibly together, of Crossraguel Abbey, in Ayrshire, where the Clerk print was taken over and adapted by Adam for his tinted view of around 1778 (figure 134, plate 9).[30] The same evolution was true of Adam's view of Cullen House where his pen and wash drawing was noted as

[28] Tait, *Landscape Garden*, p. 110.
[29] *The Gentleman's Magazine* (1792) p. 283. [30] Tait, *Master Drawings* IV, p. 53.

Figure 134 Robert Adam after John Clerk, *View of Crossraguel Abbey*

Figure 135 John Clerk, 'Castle in a landscape, after R. Adam'

based on an outline by Mr Clerk.[31] The roles were reversed, however, in the spirited, even exaggerated wash Clerk made of a typical castle landscape which was honestly acknowledged as 'J. Clerk after R. Adam' (figure 135). Such collaboration was taken a stage further when Clerk grandly presented a volume of his prints to George III in 1786. It contained sixty-two etchings, of which

[31] The drawing was noted 'No. 105 Cullen Castle / From an outline of Mr Clerks', (Blair Adam Collection, 154). A version of this drawing, without the caption is in the National Gallery of Scotland.

two were actual pen drawings by Clerk and the remainder were what the catalogue referred to as 'shaded with Indian ink upon a print out line'. It noted that they were 'tinted by Mr Robert Adam'.[32] This seems to have been limited to a judicious laying on of washes and the view of the Tower at Leith, showed the heightened effect – almost that of an aquatint – that could be achieved in this fashion (figure 136). Such sensitivity to light, shade and colour displayed in these prints was no different to Adam's reaction to recording landscape in general. It could hardly have been expected otherwise in a picturesque artist. All the landscape views and panoramas, especially the tinted ones, offered like the castles and cottages a further, perhaps deeper, insight into Adam's sympathy with the movement where architecture was treated as landscape and its visible expression contained in the landscape garden. That three of the Adam brothers were gardeners, of a sort, cannot really be doubted. James Adam wrote his *Practical Essays* from his experience as a Hertfordshire landowner and farmer, John Adam continued his father's landscaping of the familial estate at Blair Adam and Robert himself was described in 1761 as 'the best Gardener & Painter I had ever known joined in one person'.[33] Even if the surviving landscape sketchbook in New York was not a great deal more than an academic exercise under Lallemand, Adam's perspectives and plan for the park at Kedleston were a more serious contribution.

Some drawings have remained which showed, if not Adam landscape proposals, at least his sense of their need. He was fully aware of the partnership often struck between architects and gardeners, such as that of Henry Holland and Capability Brown, though both he and James Adam left the measuring and plotting of their landscapes to more practical hands. At Oxenfoord, for instance, though Robert Adam's new landscape for his rebuilt castle was shown in his print, he had left a landscape gardener, like the itinerant Thomas White, to carry out the landscape proposals shown in his various watercolour views. The text to the print strongly hinted as such circumstances in the remark that the park had 'not yet undergone all possible improvements' (figure 105).[34] Adam steered equally clear of the other provincial landscape gardeners, such as William Eames or Richard Woods, and adopted a typical Adam version of indirect control. Something of this appeared in his 1785 proposals for a castle building for the Earl of Lonsdale. He reminded his client that 'from the Back Front is seen the beautiful prospect of Hulsewater & adjacent mountains', and in his sketch proposals for The Oaks in Surrey, he recommended that the wings should be

---

[32] Tait, *Master Drawings*, IV, p. 53.

[33] Tait, *Landscape Garden*, p. 105.

[34] The text which accompanied the Oxenfoord plate referred to the landscape improvements there as not yet begun, see William Angus, *Seats of the Nobility and Gentry* (London, 1787), pl. XIV.

Figure 136   John Clerk and Robert Adam, *The Tower at Leith*

'kept back on the side towards the ground & prospect' (figure 137).[35] Where matters went further, Adam was invariably prepared to devolve authority to the man on the spot should there be a competent and experienced one available. When working in south-west Scotland, he praised Mr Dunbar of Newton Stewart as having a 'real genius for laying out of grounds about a house, and understands such trees as will thrive best in different exposures'.[36] Yet for all such devolutionary sentiments, Adam still retained overall control of the landscape as he did his buildings. Several of the perspective views he made of his houses showed that he considered their landscape setting as an essential part of his architectural creation and both clay in his hands. Such an attitude was the key to understanding the panoramas he made of Culzean, Dalquharran, or even the rustic bridge at Brasted. In every sense, they continued the tradition of the picturesque view established in *The Works* for the prints of the Syon or Bowood bridges.

In contrast, James Adam's feelings about landscape were a singular mixture of theory and practice, with a liberal dose of expediency gained from a close reading of Arthur Young's *Rural Economy* of 1770. In his *Practical Essays*, James Adam looked nostalgically back to the stout yeoman farmer of Virgil and his small-holding where, 'The Husbandman who plows his fertile land; / From troubles free, enjoys a sweet repose; / With food supply'd by nature's bounteous

---

[35] Adam's remarks on the site of the proposed Lonsdale castle are in Soane Museum AV XXXIII, f. 38. Earlier, in 1766, Robert Adam enthusiastically described the scenery as 'Cloud Capt Mountains, Extensive Lawns, Rapid Rivers and immense Forests', (Bolton, *Architecture*, II, p. 319).

[36] Bolton, *Architecture* I, p. 126.

hand'.[37] His ideal was a natural landscape where the improver or husbandman rather than the gardener dominated. The countryside had 'in my eyes', he wrote, 'far superior beauties, to the most boasted exertions of art, where silent groves are reflected by artificial rivers, and whole parishes are depopulated to pale around the boundless park, in order to indulge the sullen pomp of sequestered grandeur'.[38] From the shades of Goldsmith's Auburn, he further recommended 'the many and great advantages, in point of health, which persons employed in agriculture have over those engaged in other pursuits'.[39] If the *Practical Essays* were to be believed, he had tried out most of these lessons, in his adopted Hertfordshire, and this was confirmed by John Clerk who maintained that 'Possessing himself of a considerable farm, he made agriculture so much his study'.[40] And it may be too that his ideas on agricultural buildings influenced his brother's model farm at Culzean and added a practical element in an otherwise supremely picturesque landscape.

In the end, it seems likely that the whole gamut of the picturesque drawings existed to stimulate Robert Adam's response to an essential partnership between architecture and landscape. Such drawings widened his horizons in more than the landscape sense and encouraged him to consider his inventions as the start rather than the end of an imaginative process. The drawings of cottages and castles were, in this way, a personal account of all human endeavour, symbolised by the history of style and its evolution from the primitive huts of Laugier and Chambers. His elemental landscapes were the setting for a broad view of the past which casually mixed history and architectural history together and encouraged Adam to experiment with revival styles with a clear conscience. He was well aware that classicism, like the gothic, had a range of forms, often quite bizarre, and that in architecture rules followed invention. While he was prepared to correctly label a miniature and utilitarian Pantheon design as 'in the Roman stile' (figure 138), he was equally ready to call a bath in the Mannerist spirit of Cellini's *cinquecento* as 'in the style of the Antique', or to have designed candelabra for Luton in the style of Michelangelo (figure 94).[41] Nonetheless, Adam saw clear divisions in the history of style which made the landmarks of any period both recognisable and to an extent dateable. His handsome water-colour of 1775 for a small casino of three bays, captioned as 'In the style of an Italian Casino or Villa', was certainly a variation upon those found at Caprarola

---

[37] Adam, *Practical Essays* II, p. 515.   [38] *Ibid.*, p. 512.

[39] *Ibid.*   [40] SRO GD 18/4911, f. 134.

[41] Soane Museum, AV IV, f. 87. The drawing was dated 1744 and his continued interest in the style is shown by his pen sketch of an altar by Giovanni Bologna, presumably in Florence of 1755, Soane Museum AV LIV, series III, f. 20. For the Luton candelabra see *The Works*, part III (1775) pl. VIII. There are further drawings of sixteenth-century subjects in the Blair Adam and Clerk of Penicuik collections.

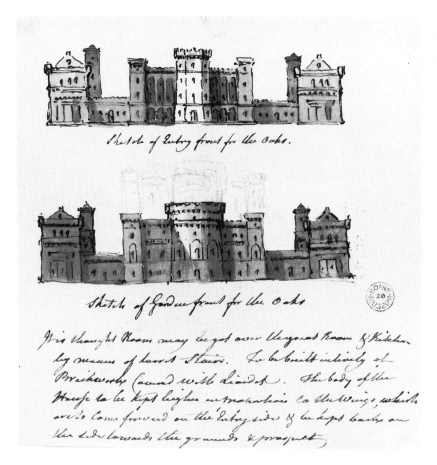

Figure 137   Robert Adam,
'Sketch for the Entry and
Garden Fronts for the Oaks'

or the Villa Lante (figure 139, plate 10).[42] Adam showed in its composition a
thorough grasp of sixteenth-century detail, which he expressed in the
rustication and relief panels of the facade as well as in the Mannerist liberties he
took with the orders. It showed both his confidence in composing in this style,
and his effective command of the underlying principles of Mannerist design. He
arranged garden vistas, changing levels and a viewing platform on the roof of the
casino with a thorough understanding of the spirit of Vignola and Ammanati
which came through in his more perfunctory design for a gardener's house at
Cullen of about 1780. A similar spirit of historicism was abroad in what Adam
termed a 'Villa Triangulaire dans le Stile Italien' (figure 140). The series of pen
drawings for it probably originated in Dewez's compositional lessons of the
1750s, as both the French title and its straightforward geometric form would

[42] Adam's visits to the Villa Lante and Caprarola were mentioned by Fleming, *Robert Adam*,
pp. 180, 230.

Figure 138 Robert Adam,
'Elevation of a Building in
the Roman Stile'

suggest.[43] There was a third scheme which can probably be added to these two
Italian essays. This was shown in a small but extraordinary pen sketch, drawn as
two alternative half-facades, of what seems to have been a precocious revival of
a Roman palace facade of the *cinquecento* (figure 141). Though undated, its sophisticated classicism was closer to the casino than the triangular villa and so part of
the picturesque experiment. Nothing seems to have come of them in their own
terms, nor was there any suggestion of such distinct revivalism in the picturesque
inventions. But the 1770s date for the casino and *palazzo* elevations was a
significant one, which highlighted Adam's widespread search during that decade

[43] See pp. 24–7.

Figure 139   Robert Adam, elevation 'in the style of an Italian Casino or Villa'

for a fresh style. In the course of the search few stones were left unturned, a fresh eye cast at his Roman drawings, and a range of styles, like his Hampton Court Jacobean, given as serious consideration as the putative *palazzo* revival.[44]

Robert Adam paid much the same thoughtful attention to the gothic. A small pen sketch he made when returning from Italy, in December 1757, was noted as 'Idée prise d'une église sur la côté de la Fleuve proche du Coblentz', and suggested that he has grasped the distinctive detail of international gothic.[45] It was an eye-catching rather than sophisticated building which possibly appealed to Adam's picturesque taste and his sympathy for its inventive, decorative style. He certainly recognised that its aims were contrary to the simple Romanesque style with which he had experimented, and he was no doubt able to see the evolution of one from the other and possibly put them in a roughly chrono-logical order. Even without such visual awareness, the historical development of the gothic had been clearly laid out already in Montfaucon's *L'Antiquité expliquée*, of which Adam owned a copy.[46] But such a narrow and scholarly approach to the gothic appealed to him as little as did a similar one to classicism and he found visual as well as historical chaos satisfying. His mixed gothic style evolved from intellectual strength rather than ignorance, and his passionate pursuit of variety and irregularity. The combining of the round and pointed arch was carried out in the same spirit as the mixture of the Greek and Roman capital, and all according to the demands of the picturesque. Just such an

[44] Soane Museum, AV LIV, series IV, f. 77.
[45] *Ibid.*, f. 2.   [46] Bolton, *Architecture*, II, p. 332.

Figure 140   Robert Adam, design for a 'Villa Trangulaire dans le Stile Italien'

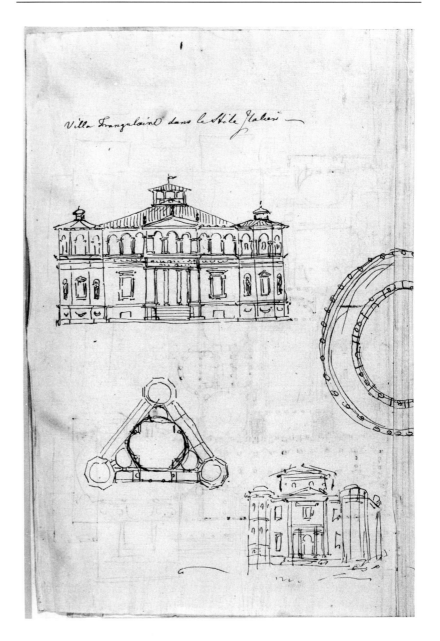

extraordinary hybrid was the very late design of 1792 for a church which Adam teasingly captioned as a 'Building in the Morisk stile like the Church at Kelso' (figure 142). Yet his attitude was serious rather than solemn, and his design was principally taken from the remaining north transept of the Abbey which inspired the pattern he adopted of buttresses topped by small, round towers. The detailing of Adam's recessed western door, the simple round-headed windows

Figure 141   Robert Adam,
*Alternative designs for a palazzo
style facade*

Figure 142   Robert Adam,
'Building in the Morisk stile
like the Church at Kelso'

and the bold string courses were all similarly derived, though Adam's central
tower and spire (with clock) were only the loosest possible interpretation of the
existing lantern. In such a mixture with its casual reference to a Moorish
evolution, Robert Adam was indulging to the full his picturesque vocabulary as
well as provoking the antiquarian and classicist alike. A comparable eclectic

167

Figure 143 James Adam,
'Church for the Heritors of
the Barony Parish Glasgow'

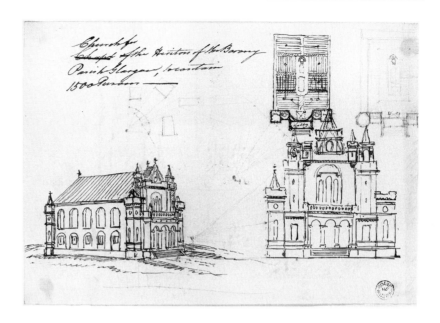

Figure 143 James Adam, 'Church for the Heritors of the Barony Parish Glasgow'

spirit appeared two years later in James Adam's Barony Church, his Glasgow swansong of 1794 (figure 143).

Whether Robert Adam saw all his styles and revivals as variations of equal weight, or whether he accepted them as sorts of architectural horses for courses, is possibly neither here nor there. In the pursuit of the picturesque, variety and novelty were the essence. Adam was increasingly concerned to develop architecture as an almost intuitive response of the imagination rather than intellect, and as a variation on the concept of a sixth sense of innate good taste. Throughout his career, he remained sceptical, if not hostile, to the insistence that truth was to be found in the purity of one style alone. This, undoubtedly, led him to run a range of styles as far apart and as extreme as the Chinese, gothic and Egyptian, and to extend his antiquarian interest from the Etruscan of Piranesi to the gothic of Montfaucon. The picturesque was probably the ideal vehicle for such an open mind and this gave Adam unquestionable freedom from the orthodox notions of style that he had found so stifling and deadening.

Though Robert Adam was prepared to change his labels from time to time, the pattern was nonetheless a remarkably consistent one. His faith in the picturesque never wavered. The youthful enthusiasm for landscape of his Blair Adam days grew during his Italian years and was matched by his talent to capture in drawing and watercolour the variety and mood of the picturesque. This certainly underpinned his conservative stance in the Graeco–Roman controversy and equally so his brand of allusive classicism, practised so successfully during the sixties. The turning point was the appearance of *The*

Works in 1773, which signalled, as the way forward, the concept of architecture as scenery and the indivisible bond between drawing, building and planting. In this concluding phase of his career, Robert Adam's genius as a watercolourist or tinter of his inventions was of the utmost importance. It offered the drawings as the key as much to his architecture as to his imagination.

Index